OPPOSING
VIEWPOINTS®
SERIES

The
Palestinian Territories

Other Books of Related Interest:

At Issue Series
Is China's Economic Growth a Threat to America?
Should the US Close Its Borders?

Current Controversies Series
Islamophobia
Pakistan

Introducing Issues with Opposing Viewpoints Series
The Taliban

Opposing Viewpoints Series
Multiracial America
North Korea and South Korea

"Congress shall make no law . . . abridging the freedom of speech, or of the press."

First Amendment to the US Constitution

The basic foundation of our democracy is the First Amendment guarantee of freedom of expression. The Opposing Viewpoints series is dedicated to the concept of this basic freedom and the idea that it is more important to practice it than to enshrine it.

OPPOSING
VIEWPOINTS®
SERIES

The
Palestinian Territories

Margaret Haerens, Book Editor

GREENHAVEN PRESS
A part of Gale, Cengage Learning

GALE
CENGAGE Learning·

Farmington Hills, Mich • San Francisco • New York • Waterville, Maine
Meriden, Conn • Mason, Ohio • Chicago

Elizabeth Des Chenes, *Director, Content Strategy*
Douglas Dentino, *Manager, New Product*

© 2014 Greenhaven Press, a part of Gale, Cengage Learning

WCN: 01-100-101

LIBRARY OF CONGRESS CATALOGING-IN-PUBLICATION DATA

The Palestinian territories / Margaret Haerens, book editor.
    pages cm. -- (Opposing viewpoints)
    Includes bibliographical references and index.
    ISBN 978-0-7377-6967-8 (hardcover) -- ISBN 978-0-7377-6968-5 (pbk.)
    1. Palestine—International status. 2. Palestine—Politics and government. 3. Palestinian Arabs—Politics and government. 4. Arab-Israeli conflict—1993—Peace. I. Haerens, Margaret, editor of compilation.
    DS119.76.P359 2014
    956.95'3044—dc23
                                                            2013047321

Printed in the United States of America
1 2 3 4 5 6 7 18 17 16 15 14

Contents

Chapter 3: How Can Circumstances in the Palestinian Territories Be Improved?

Chapter 4: How Should the United States Treat the Palestinian Territories?

Why Consider Opposing Viewpoints?

> *"The only way in which a human being can make some approach to knowing the whole of a subject is by hearing what can be said about it by persons of every variety of opinion and studying all modes in which it can be looked at by every character of mind. No wise man ever acquired his wisdom in any mode but this."*
>
> *John Stuart Mill*

In our media-intensive culture it is not difficult to find differing opinions. Thousands of newspapers and magazines and dozens of radio and television talk shows resound with differing points of view. The difficulty lies in deciding which opinion to agree with and which "experts" seem the most credible. The more inundated we become with differing opinions and claims, the more essential it is to hone critical reading and thinking skills to evaluate these ideas. Opposing Viewpoints books address this problem directly by presenting stimulating debates that can be used to enhance and teach these skills. The varied opinions contained in each book examine many different aspects of a single issue. While examining these conveniently edited opposing views, readers can develop critical thinking skills such as the ability to compare and contrast authors' credibility, facts, argumentation styles, use of persuasive techniques, and other stylistic tools. In short, the Opposing Viewpoints Series is an ideal way to attain the higher-level thinking and reading skills so essential in a culture of diverse and contradictory opinions.

In addition to providing a tool for critical thinking, Opposing Viewpoints books challenge readers to question their own strongly held opinions and assumptions. Most people form their opinions on the basis of upbringing, peer pressure, and personal, cultural, or professional bias. By reading carefully balanced opposing views, readers must directly confront new ideas as well as the opinions of those with whom they disagree. This is not to argue simplistically that everyone who reads opposing views will—or should—change his or her opinion. Instead, the series enhances readers' understanding of their own views by encouraging confrontation with opposing ideas. Careful examination of others' views can lead to the readers' understanding of the logical inconsistencies in their own opinions, perspective on why they hold an opinion, and the consideration of the possibility that their opinion requires further evaluation.

Evaluating Other Opinions

To ensure that this type of examination occurs, Opposing Viewpoints books present all types of opinions. Prominent spokespeople on different sides of each issue as well as well-known professionals from many disciplines challenge the reader. An additional goal of the series is to provide a forum for other, less known, or even unpopular viewpoints. The opinion of an ordinary person who has had to make the decision to cut off life support from a terminally ill relative, for example, may be just as valuable and provide just as much insight as a medical ethicist's professional opinion. The editors have two additional purposes in including these less known views. One, the editors encourage readers to respect others' opinions—even when not enhanced by professional credibility. It is only by reading or listening to and objectively evaluating others' ideas that one can determine whether they are worthy of consideration. Two, the inclusion of such viewpoints encourages the important critical thinking skill of objectively evaluating an author's credentials and bias. This evaluation will illuminate an author's reasons for taking a particular stance on an issue and will aid in readers' evaluation of the author's ideas.

It is our hope that these books will give readers a deeper understanding of the issues debated and an appreciation of the complexity of even seemingly simple issues when good and honest people disagree. This awareness is particularly important in a democratic society such as ours in which people enter into public debate to determine the common good. Those with whom one disagrees should not be regarded as enemies but rather as people whose views deserve careful examination and may shed light on one's own.

Thomas Jefferson once said that "difference of opinion leads to inquiry, and inquiry to truth." Jefferson, a broadly educated man, argued that "if a nation expects to be ignorant and free . . . it expects what never was and never will be." As individuals and as a nation, it is imperative that we consider the opinions of others and examine them with skill and discernment. The Opposing Viewpoints series is intended to help readers achieve this goal.

David L. Bender and Bruno Leone,
Founders

Introduction

"Like people everywhere, Palestinians deserve a future of hope—that their rights will be respected, that tomorrow will be better than today, and that they can give their children a life of dignity and opportunity. Put simply, Palestinians deserve a state of their own."

—US president
Barack Obama

The origins of today's Israeli-Palestinian conflict can be traced back to the late nineteenth century, when both Palestinian and Zionist nationalist groups began to gain popularity and garner global support. At the time, the region that would later become Israel and the Palestinian Territories was ruled by the Turkish Ottoman Empire and was populated by Arab Muslims, known as Palestinians, and small concentrations of Jews and Christians. As the power of the Ottoman Empire began to decline at the end of the nineteenth century, Zionism, the movement in Europe to establish a Jewish homeland, facilitated the migration of a growing number of European Jews to the major cities in the region.

The Ottomans were on the losing side in World War I (1914–1918), after which the British took control of Palestine. In 1922 the League of Nations approved the British Mandate of Palestine, an agreement among several world powers that the British would keep administrative control of the territory. During the 1930s, there was a mass immigration of European Jews into Palestine, escaping from a rising tide of anti-Semitism generated by the growing power of Adolf Hitler and the Nazi Party in Germany. The mass migration alarmed many Palestinian Arabs in the British Mandate and sparked a strong

Palestinian nationalist movement. From 1936 to 1939 there were a series of Arab revolts to end British rule and establish a Palestinian state in the region.

British officials convened a public inquiry, known as the Peel Commission, in response to the revolts. The commission recommended that a Jewish territory be established in the Galilee region and along the western coast of the British Mandate. Palestinian Arabs rejected the recommendations and the violence against Jewish settlers continued.

The White Paper of 1939, a policy paper released by the British government, reassessed the future of British Palestine and recommended the creation of a Palestinian state governed by both Palestinians and Jews. Both Palestinian and Jewish groups rejected the proposal.

During World War II, the British policy of restricting the number of European Jews migrating to the region led to waves of illegal immigrations and a growing resentment from Zionist groups. By 1947, the British were ready to relinquish control of the region and turned to the United Nations to broker a resolution.

On November 29, 1947, the United Nations General Assembly passed Resolution 181, which recommended that British Palestine be partitioned into independent Jewish and Arabic states. Jerusalem, recognized as a holy site for Muslims, Jews, and Christians, would be administered by the United Nations. Zionist leaders accepted the proposed plan, but Arab leaders rejected it.

In the following months, sectarian violence between Arabs and Jews exploded into a civil war, which became known as the 1948 Palestine War. After a number of military successes, Zionist forces announced the establishment of the State of Israel on May 14, 1948—the same day the British Mandate over Palestine expired. Israel was immediately recognized by several world powers, including both the Soviet Union and the United States.

The civil war continued, however, with several neighboring Arab states lending support to the Palestinian forces. However, the Israeli forces continued to win military victories and began to push into territory earmarked for the proposed Palestinian state. A cease-fire and armistice agreements were implemented in 1949, and the region was reallocated between Israel and its Arab neighbors: Israel retained the land that the United Nations had allotted to it and added a large area that Israel had captured during the war; Jordan occupied the West Bank; the city of Jerusalem was split between Israel and Jordan; and Egypt took control of the Gaza Strip, where it installed and oversaw an All-Palestine government. Many observers consider this government to be the first attempt to establish an independent Palestinian state. In 1959, the All-Palestine government in Gaza was subsumed into the United Arab Republic, a political union between Egypt and Syria, which was a major setback for the Palestinian nationalist movement.

Tensions between Israel and its Arab neighbors continued to build throughout the 1960s. Much of the hostility in the region was rooted in questions of Israel's legitimacy and the belief of Arabs in the region that there should be an independent Palestinian state. Surrounded by antagonistic neighbors, Israel was motivated by its own determination to survive and successfully defend itself against waves of ruthless and deadly terrorist attacks, often supported by Arab countries in the Middle East.

In June 1967 a minor border skirmish between Israel and Syria sparked the Six-Day War, which involved Israel, Syria, Egypt, and Jordan. By the time a ceasefire was called, Israel had conquered several new territories, including the Sinai Peninsula and the Gaza Strip from Egypt; East Jerusalem and the West Bank from Jordan; and the Golan Heights from Syria.

In November 1967 the United Nations passed Resolution 242, which called for Israel's withdrawal from the territories it captured during the Six-Day War in exchange for peace with its neighbors. With the help of the United States, the Israelis and Egyptians were finally able to negotiate a peace agreement in 1979, known as the Camp David Accords. As a result, the Sinai was returned to Egyptian control in exchange for a cessation of hostility between the two countries.

During this time, Palestinian groups were launching terrorist attacks within and outside of Israel. In response, the Israel Defense Forces (IDF) launched widespread crackdowns on Palestinian militants and implemented policies that had a destructive economic, political, cultural, and social effect on Palestinian society. Many Palestinians were detained, deported, or killed, and the homes of thousands of Palestinians were demolished to make room for Israeli settlements. Life in the region for Palestinians was characterized by rising unemployment, rampant poverty, and widespread discrimination.

In 1987 the frustrations of the Palestinian people led to the First Intifada, a violent uprising against Israeli subjugation. Palestinians employed a number of measures during the Intifada, including economic boycotts of Israeli businesses and products, civil disobedience, throwing stones at military vehicles, and even suicide bombings.

After the 1991 Gulf War, the United States began diplomatic efforts to jump-start peace talks between Israel and the Palestinians. The Madrid negotiations of 1991 led to the Oslo Accords of 1993, which called for the IDF to withdraw from the West Bank and Gaza to allow for Palestinian self-government by the Palestinian National Authority (usually referred to as the Palestinian Authority, or PA). Also, the Palestine Liberation Organization (PLO), a former terrorist group and the most powerful political faction among the Palestinian people, would be recognized as the central Palestinian authority, and its leader, Yasser Arafat, would be allowed to return to the West Bank. In return, the PLO would renounce violence and acknowledge the state of Israel.

In the following years, there would be additional efforts to advance the peace process and establish a Palestinian state. Many of those efforts have been derailed by continued violence, political intransigence, and a lack of international pressure. In the early twenty-first century, there was a renewed push at the United Nations to recognize the state of Palestine in hopes that such recognition would reignite negotiations for a two-state (Israel and Palestine) solution in the region.

On November 29, 2012, the United Nations General Assembly voted to grant Palestine nonmember observer state status in the United Nations. The victory was a symbolic one for the Palestinians, who had been rejected for full member-state status in the United Nations in 2011. The 2012 vote cemented Palestine's legitimacy with the United Nations and a majority of its member states and signaled overwhelming international support for an independent Palestinian state.

The implementation of a two-state solution will continue to be a pressing issue in any resolution to the Israeli-Palestinian conflict. The authors of the viewpoints in *Opposing Viewpoints: The Palestinian Territories* debate the solutions to the problems of the region in the following chapters: What Is the Best Solution to the Palestinian-Israeli Conflict?, Should the United Nations Grant Palestinian Statehood?, How Can Circumstances in the Palestinian Territories Be Improved?, and How Should the United States Treat the Palestinian Territories? After more than fifty years of conflict-ridden existence, Israel and the Palestinians have not resolved their differences. The viewpoints in this volume update the reader on the intransigent issues facing these intractable enemies.

OPPOSING
VIEWPOINTS®
SERIES

CHAPTER 1

What Is the Best Solution to the Palestinian-Israeli Conflict?

Chapter Preface

On June 5, 1967, Israel launched a war in the Middle East by preemptively striking Egyptian forces that were planning an attack on Israel. Within days, both Jordan and Syria had joined Egypt in the battle against Israel. The battle would last only six days and end with Israel achieving significant military and political victories. Not only did Israel seize key territory from Egypt, Jordan, and Syria, it also showed the world that it was fully capable of standing its ground and protecting itself against its enemies. The battle, which would come to be known as the Six-Day War, or the Arab-Israeli War of 1967, also paved the way for later disputes over the Palestinian Territories and the possible boundaries of an independent Palestinian state.

Since its establishment in 1948, Israel has had frequent conflicts with its Arab neighbors. The central dispute centers around questions of Israel's right to exist. At that time, a solid majority of Arabs in the region believed that the territory given to Israel rightfully belonged to the Palestinian people, not the Jewish people. They vowed to destroy Israel and create a Palestinian state in its place. Such a deep-seated conflict—based in and exacerbated by history, religion, economics, politics, and social issues—was a daunting diplomatic challenge and a consistent threat to Israel's continued existence.

By the mid-1960s, tension between Israel and its Arab neighbors, as well as the Palestinian Arabs living within its borders, had elevated to a boiling point. Israel's decision to cultivate an area for agricultural purposes in the demilitarized zone between Syria and Israel led to a military skirmish between the two powers on April 7, 1967—and sparked a series of events that would lead to the Six-Day War.

Alarmed by false reports that Israel was amassing troops at the border of Syria for an imminent attack, Egypt decided to protect its Syrian ally and closed the Strait of Tiran, an international waterway located between the Sinai and Arabian Peninsulas, to all shipping to and from Israel on May 21, 1967. Israel regarded this as an act of war. Diplomatic efforts failed to soothe the escalating tensions in the region.

On the morning of June 5, the Israeli military launched Operation Focus, a surprise air strike on the Egyptian Air Force that destroyed a number of key Egyptian airfields and matériel. Over the next few days, the Israeli military launched successful offensive campaigns against Egyptian forces on the Sinai Peninsula and the Gaza Strip as well as against the Jordanian military in East Jerusalem and the West Bank (of the Jordan River). The war ended with major battles against the Syrian forces in the Golan Heights. On June 11, a ceasefire was signed and the Six-Day War ended. It was a resounding victory for Israel, which had captured several new territories: the Sinai Peninsula and the Gaza Strip from Egypt; East Jerusalem and the West Bank from Jordan; and the Golan Heights from Syria. (The Sinai was eventually returned to Egyptian control as part of the 1979 peace agreement between Egypt and Israel.)

In November 1967 the United Nations passed Resolution 242, which called for Israel's withdrawal from the territories it captured during the Six-Day War in exchange for peace with its neighbors. Known as the land-for-peace formula, it has served as the basis for Arab-Israeli peace negotiations for years.

Today, there is a growing campaign to establish an independent Palestine based on the pre-1967 borders of Israel. That means that a Palestinian state would be made up of Israeli-occupied territories captured in the Six-Day War: the West Bank, Gaza Strip, East Jerusalem, and the Golan Heights. Israel has rejected the idea, arguing that it is not realistic to think that it can withdraw to pre-1967 borders after years of population growth and new settlements in the so-called Palestinian Territories.

The negotiations of the possible borders of a new Palestinian state is one of the issues discussed in the following chapter, which explores the best solutions to the Palestinian-Israeli conflict. Other viewpoints in the chapter analyze the debate over the one-state and two-state solutions, the viability of two-state condominialism, and the necessity of eliminating discrimination against the Palestinian people in any solution to the conflict.

| *"There is no serious alternative to a two-state deal."*

The Two-State Solution Should Be Implemented

The Economist

The Economist is a weekly news and international affairs publication based in the United Kingdom. In the following viewpoint, the author chronicles the rising trend among Israel's right-wing politicians, frustrated Palestinians, and various academics and commentators to support a one-state solution to the Israeli-Palestinian problem. This increasingly popular proposal would keep the region under Israel's control but provide equal rights for all citizens and a level of autonomy in Palestinian areas. This is a mistake, the author contends, because a one-state solution would never work. Palestinians would never be content with living under Israeli rule. In addition, Jews will eventually be a minority in the region if current population trends continue, which would lead to the Jews being outnumbered and outvoted by the Palestinians. The only serious solution to the Israeli-Palestinian conflict is the two-state idea.

"Could Two Become One?," *The Economist*, March 16, 2013. Reproduced with permission.

As you read, consider the following questions:

1. In what year did Israel's prime minister, Benjamin Netanyahu, give a speech in which he endorsed the two-state solution, according to *The Economist*?

2. According to the author, what is the position of Israel's Labour Party on the two-state solution?

3. How many Palestinians live in the West Bank, according to population estimates cited by the author?

In 1942, as the Holocaust in Europe was entering its most horrific phase, a pacifist American rabbi called Judah Magnes helped found a political party in Palestine called Ihud. Hebrew for unity, Ihud argued for a single binational state in the Holy Land to be shared by Jews and Arabs. Its efforts—and those of like-minded idealists—came to naught. Bitterly opposed to the partition of Palestine, Magnes died in 1948 just as the state of Israel—the *naqba*, or catastrophe, to Palestinians—was being born. Decades of strife were to follow.

At the United Nations, in the White House and around the world, there is a strong belief that any solution ending that strife must be based on two separate states, with a mainly Jewish one called Israel sitting alongside a mainly Arab one called Palestine. The border between them would be based on the one that existed before the 1967 war—known as the "green line"—with some adjustments and land swaps to reflect the world as it is. Jerusalem would be a shared but divided capital.

In the face of the manifold obstacles facing such a solution, however, something like Magnes's one-state variant has been coming back into vogue, both in left-wing Western (and Jewish) circles and among a growing minority of Palestinians. In 2004 a British-born Israeli writer, Daniel Gavron, published a book, *The Other Side of Despair: Jews and Arabs in the Promised Land*, that called for the creation of a democratic binational "State of Jerusalem". Some Israeli intellectuals are airing the notion of "Post-Zionism". Avraham Burg, a former Speaker of the Knesset, Israel's Parliament, says a "post-national" model must be explored. "I have no doubt something is emerging, though I am not sure what it is."

One but Not the Same

Avi Shlaim, a leading British chronicler of the Israel-Palestine saga who was born in Baghdad and brought up in Israel, says he has "shifted . . . to supporting a one-state solution with equal rights for all citizens," though he concedes that "this is not what I would ideally like." Past and present Israeli governments, he thinks, have killed the two-state option, partly by entrenching Jewish settlements so deeply on the West Bank, the heartland of a would-be Palestinian state, that they cannot be removed.

This is an assessment the idealists share with hawkish Israelis and a growing number of Palestinians. More and more often, the two-state solution is pronounced dead. Mathematics suggests that the alternative is a one-state solution. But though there are a lot of different one-state outcomes under discussion, none of them really looks like a solution.

If one state is simply the rejection of two states, then many Israelis on the right are up for it. In 2009, under American pressure, Israel's prime minister, Binyamin Netanyahu, gave a speech at Bar-Ilan University in which he grudgingly endorsed the two-state idea. Since then he has shown barely a flicker of enthusiasm for it. In a speech to the American Congress in May 2011, he declared triumphantly, and to sustained applause, that Jerusalem would be undivided, evidently under Israeli control, noting that "the vast majority of the 650,000 Israelis who live beyond the 1967 lines reside in neighbourhoods and suburbs of Jerusalem and Greater Tel Aviv." Yet it is barely conceivable that the Palestinians would ever accept a state that excluded all of Jerusalem.

Mr Netanyahu has made clear that he will not countenance the bulk of the West Bank's settlers being pushed out in order to let the Palestinians have their state. And he is emphatic that Israel must control the Jordan valley as well as the airspace above the Palestinians; their West Bank state would exist under an Israeli lid. "He never made a clear-cut commitment to the two-state solution," says Mr Netanyahu's predecessor as prime minister, Ehud Olmert.

Regardless of Mr Netanyahu's position, his Likud party has refused to endorse the creation of any kind of Palestinian state. Most of its Knesset members have joined a "Greater Israel Caucus" that says the West Bank must stay part of Israel for ever. Avigdor Lieberman, a rough-hewn populist whose largely ethnic-Russian party merged with Likud before the election, backs partition but also wants to encourage the fifth of Israeli citizens who are Arabs living within Israel's 1967 boundary to leave—ethnic cleansing, in Palestinian eyes. Arab Israelis who fail a "test of loyalty" to the state of Israel should, he says, be deprived of various rights, such as the vote. Mr Lieberman is currently out of office, pending an investigation into alleged fraud, but the 31 seats held together by his party and Likud is easily the biggest bloc in the 120-seat Knesset.

You Gave Me Nothing

Naftali Bennett, a 40-year-old software tycoon with a hip Californian manner, is the most strident new voice on the Israeli right: blunter than Mr Netanyahu, more openly dismissive of the two-state idea, and more hawkish than another, bigger beneficiary of Israeli voters in January's [2013] general election, Yair Lapid. (Mr Lapid's party won 19 seats in the Knesset to Mr Bennett's 12.) Asked about removing Jewish settlements from the West Bank and creating a Palestinian state between Jerusalem and the Jordan river, Mr Bennett breezily replies that "It just ain't gonna happen." Of the Palestinians, he says

"I will do everything in my power to make sure they never get a state. It would be national suicide for Israel."

Instead, Mr Bennett wants Israel to annex the 61% of the West Bank known as "Area C", in essence the territory's central and eastern slab, going down to the Jordan valley. The Palestinians—at least 50,000—who live there would become Israeli citizens, should they stay. The other 2.6m or so Palestinians on the West Bank would have to be content with "full-blown autonomy" in their towns and villages. This, in essence, would mean municipal rights (he mentions garbage collection). Jewish settlers would stay put.

Mr Lapid, a jovial former television anchorman now deemed a kingmaker in the Knesset, is considered a centrist by Israelis. But he is no enthusiast for a two-state plan, at least not of the sort promoted by Western diplomats or in the UN. He chose to make his chief election speech at the university of Ariel, one of the largest and most controversial of Jewish settlements, a town of 20,000 people (with another 12,000 students) built deep within the West Bank. The second person on his party's list in the Knesset is a settler rabbi. Mr Lapid also argues for Jerusalem to remain undivided under Israeli control.

Support for a Two-State Idea

The only mainly Jewish parties that treat negotiations towards a two-state solution as a priority are Tzipi Livni's group (which won a paltry six seats in the recent election), Meretz (which also got six) and the rump of Ariel Sharon's Kadima party (just two). Three Arab-Israeli parties, all two-staters, got 11 seats between them.

The Labour Party, long Israel's leading proponent of a two-state solution, got 15 seats. But its campaign concentrated almost exclusively on domestic issues. Indeed, the degree to which the election and its coalition-cobbling aftermath ignored negotiations with the Palestinians to any end at all was telling. Mr Bennett's provocative no-state-for-the-Palestinians oratory was noticed. But he was never rebuked for it by, say, Mr Netanyahu.

In sum, despite Mr Netanyahu's glum espousal of the two-state idea in his speech at Bar-Ilan, proponents of a state of Israel that encompasses all or most of the West Bank are plainly the strongest force in the Knesset. On March 14th [2013], Mr Netanyahu announced a proposed government in advance of a visit by [US president] Barack Obama on March 20th. It contains Mr Lapid and Mr Bennett; Ms Livni will probably be its only member keenly committed to negotiations with the Palestinians.

Within Israel, the Palestinian question simply does not seem urgent. Even the settlers do not seem to feel threatened. With a web of well-built roads knitting their infrastructure into that of Israel proper—some of them reserved for Israeli use—a visitor barely notices which side of the green line he is on. Those living in the settlements have scant contact with Palestinians whose villages lie close by. In 2012, for the first year since 1973, not a single Jewish Israeli was killed as a result of Palestinian violence on the West Bank.

The South African Comparison

Palestinians, for their part, talk more and more of "a one-state reality"—while most caution that it is not a "solution". They argue that the notion of a viable, contiguous, sovereign Palestinian state sitting peacefully alongside Israel is no longer feasible. An ever more popular parallel for the situation is South Africa before and after its emergence from apartheid.

The main similarity is the existence of two separate systems of government and law for two people living side by side on territory that is occupied as a result of conquest and confiscation. The web of Israeli roads and the restrictions that Palestinians face in terms of travel are compared to the se-

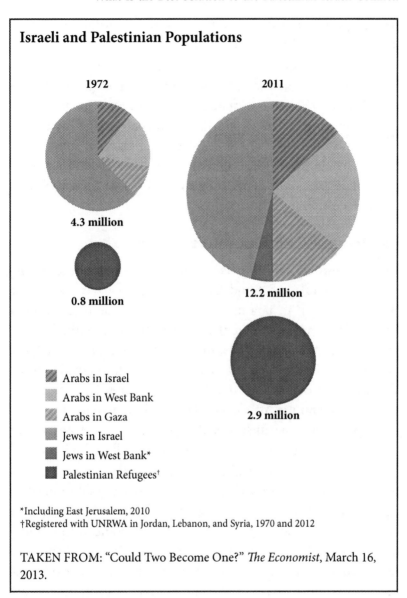

Israeli and Palestinian Populations

1972

2011

4.3 million

0.8 million

12.2 million

2.9 million

▨ Arabs in Israel
▨ Arabs in West Bank
▨ Arabs in Gaza
▨ Jews in Israel
▨ Jews in West Bank*
▨ Palestinian Refugees†

*Including East Jerusalem, 2010
†Registered with UNRWA in Jordan, Lebanon, and Syria, 1970 and 2012

TAKEN FROM: "Could Two Become One?" *The Economist*, March 16, 2013.

questering of black South Africans in wretched "bantustans". Israel's security fence, in many places a five-metre (15-foot) concrete wall wound round Jewish settlements is inevitably known to Palestinians as "the apartheid wall". Scores of checkpoints recall the old South African "pass laws" whereby blacks needed permission to go from one area to another, especially in search of work in "white" areas.

The campaign for Boycott, Divestment and Sanctions (BDS) against Israel, which is growing in strength in America and Britain, sees the one-state reality as a precursor to a civil-rights movement that would then bring down the "apartheid state" with the help, as in South Africa, of external support inflamed by the injustice. If Jewish settlers were determined to remain on the West Bank, they might be able to do so—but under Palestinian authority.

To Drag the Past Out into the Light

Israel's president, Shimon Peres, and its former prime ministers Ehud Barak and Ehud Olmert—men in what used to be the mainstream of national politics—worry about just such a future. They have warned that, unless the occupation of the bulk of the West Bank ends, or Palestinians in the West Bank are given full voting rights in Israel, the country will lose its claim to be a democracy. It will, says Mr Peres, become a "pariah", just as South Africa did. The BDS campaign may thus, he implies, become unstoppable. Even the Americans might find it hard to go on backing Israel come hell or high water.

More hawkish Palestinians, typified by the Islamist movement, Hamas, are not giving up on a two-state solution; they never believed in it in the first place. They still dream of a land where they hold sway from the Mediterranean to the Jordan river, with Jews and Christians living there, if they are lucky, on sufferance. Accepting that this harsh scenario is unlikely to come to pass in the short run, its proponents talk merrily of the long game, waiting for a generation or even two.

These true-believing one-staters have a strong position in Hamas, and it is one that will likely get stronger if people like Mr Bennett call the Israeli tune. "We consider the whole of Palestine our land," says Mahmoud Zahar, a Hamas leader in

Gaza, sitting at home beside a portrait of two sons killed fighting the Israelis. History and time, he says with a big smile, are on Hamas's side. "The Islamic trend is coming to power. Ten years is enough to neutralise the power of Israel and its supporters." An Islamist regime has come to power next-door in Egypt; Syria may be next; Hamas's allies in Jordan are shaking King Abdullah's throne. "No one can guess what will happen tomorrow."

"In the end I am sure there will be just one state," says Basam al-Naim, for seven years Hamas's minister of health in Gaza. "But what kind of state I cannot say. Many Jews would leave and many Palestinians would come back. In ten to 20 years there will be a completely different geopolitical map." The [1 million]-odd Russian Jews who have bolstered Israel since the Soviet Union collapsed, he says, would have to go. "They are already segregated in Israel," he adds. "And many of them are not even Jews."

Over the years, some Hamas leaders, such as Khaled Meshal, have groped towards accepting Israel, at least as a "reality" to be grudgingly accepted. Some now posit a two-state solution, albeit often as a step on the way to a single state, once Muslims, Jews and Christians learn to live happily together, perhaps in some federal halfway house.

No Clear-Cut Solution

In every one-state outcome, be it created by virtue of persuasion or under duress, Jews would eventually be a minority. Mr Bennett seeks to avoid this by advocating "autonomy" outside Israel for much of the West Bank. But he must know that the autonomy he advocates will never satisfy the Palestinians, nor the neighbouring Arab countries that host several million Palestinian refugees, most of whose forebears fled when Israel was founded in 1948. "I do not have a clear-cut solution," he concedes, before reverting to the old argument that "Jordan is Palestine." Most Jordanians, it is true, are of Palestinian origin.

But would Palestinians on the West Bank and in Gaza, let alone those within the borders of Israel, be satisfied with a state on the east side of the Jordan river, presuming that the present monarchy would grant it to them? Not a chance. Though Mr Bennett might want them to, the Egyptians aren't going to let Gaza be dumped on them, either.

But, like the activists of BDS, Mr Bennett and his friends know that granting Palestinians proper civil rights within an enlarged Israel would mean that the Jews would soon be outnumbered and later outvoted by the Palestinians. Though ultra-Orthodox Jews are the fastest growing community in Israel, Palestinians still outbreed Israelis as a whole. Palestinians in Israel already add up to 1.6m, along with 2.6m on the West Bank and 1.7m in Gaza. Jewish Israelis on both sides of the green line number about 6m. "In ten to 15 years Palestinians would have a majority in one state," says Mr Olmert.

This means that none of the one-state options makes sense for Israel in the long run. The idealists paint a picture of Arabs and Jews getting along swimmingly together: dream on. The hawks think the Palestinians can be kept quiet for ever if they are denied a state: again, dream on.

At the same time, the analogy with South Africa is fatally flawed. Israel within its 1967 borders has international legitimacy; no white South African state could ever have claimed as much; beyond a few Afrikaner zealots the idea would have been a non-starter. So a two-state solution was never possible. And a situation in which blacks outnumber whites by ten to one is completely unlike a situation where the sides have comparable numbers. In conceding the principle of one-person-one-vote South Africa's whites knew that they were losing their political primacy for good. Israeli Jews will not do that.

Do You Feel the Same?

Even if the Palestinians were remarkably tolerant—and that is questionable—Israel as a Jewish state would disappear. Even the name would go. It is barely conceivable that Jews, after running their own vibrant polity for half a century and praying for a return to their ancestral homeland for two millennia, would quietly submit to Palestinian majority rule, however idealistic its proponents. That is why Dov Khenin, a Jewish member of the Knesset's mainly Arab and communist-inclined Hadash party, sees two states as the only practical path to peace even while sympathising with the ideals of the one-staters. "If the two peoples want to have a binational state, OK," he says wistfully. "But my impression is that Israelis and Palestinians don't very much like each other." Nor, he implies, will they ever do so.

Academic gatherings, such as a conference last year [2012] at Harvard to discuss the one-state option, have yet to put flesh on the idealists' notions. Would a federal framework provide for separate assemblies? What sort of army and police would there be? Would, as Mr Gavron's book suggests, the Jews have to drop their Law of Return (allowing any diaspora Jew to become a citizen) and the Palestinians likewise have to drop their Right of Return (letting all refugees and their descendants back)? Few have begun to address such nettlesome questions, because in truth, few see a one-state outcome as a true goal. Most come to it out of exhausted despair or amiable fantasy.

Israel, as Mr Netanyahu must know, cannot remain both democratic and Jewish if it continues to control several million Palestinians without granting them full political rights. At the same time, he dreads the encirclement of hostile Arab states around him, and frets that America, under Barack Obama, may fail to make good on its promise to prevent Iran from getting a nuclear bomb. Meanwhile he lamely repeats the old mantra that "there is no Palestinian partner for peace."

Quite possibly he does not know what he should, can or will do. Had [2012 Republican candidate] Mitt Romney won the American presidency, he might have given Mr Netanyahu a fillip [a smack]. Mr Obama has no such desire. Instead, he will repeat to the Israeli leader what Mr Netanyahu has almost said but cannot bring himself fully to endorse—that there is no serious alternative to a two-state deal.

| *"Today's Israel-Palestine is demonstrably one state, impossible to divide."*

A One-State Solution Should Be Implemented

Ghada Karmi

Ghada Karmi is a Palestinian activist, academic, and writer. In the following viewpoint, she deems a two-state solution to the Israeli-Palestinian crisis to be unattainable in light of current realities; She thus presses for a wholesale reassessment of Palestinian political strategy. The only realistic solution, Karmi argues, is one state with equal rights for all citizens. Under this strategy, Palestinians would be able to address the gross economic and social equality that has hindered progress and the human rights violations that have devastated individuals, families, and communities. A one-state solution would also fully expose Israel's discriminatory and even brutal occupation of the Palestinian people and force meaningful political and social reform in the region, she maintains.

As you read, consider the following questions:

1. According to the author, by how much has donor funding to the Palestinian Authority declined?

2. How much of the West Bank land is controlled by Israel, according to Karmi?

3. If a one-state solution were implemented, how many new Arab citizens of Israel does Karmi say there would be?

It is one year this week [late September 2012] since the Palestinians applied for UN membership. President Mahmoud Abbas's impassioned plea to the UN's General Assembly for support of the We Palestinian case on 23 September 2011 won him much praise, even from his detractors. But it came to nothing, and no further Palestinian application for UN membership was made. Now, however, the statehood issue is back on the Palestinian agenda.

Abbas has recently threatened to relaunch the UN application if Israeli settlement expansion continues. This time he would seek UN non-member observer state status, but has yet to decide to consult with Arab and other states, and it may come to nothing again. Only a bankruptcy of ideas could be driving him towards this move, given the present situation of US acquiescence to regional Israeli hegemony, and Israel's stunning success in diverting world attention from the conflict on its doorstep to Iran's nonexistent nuclear weapons.

The president also faces serious trouble at home. The Palestinian economy, dependent on aid, is staggering under a chronic budget deficit and external debt of a billion dollars, nearly a fifth of GDP [gross domestic product]. Donor funding has declined from $1 billion to $750 million, and the Palestinian Authority [PA] has delayed paying 153,000 employees, prompting protests. Mass strikes and demonstrations have rocked the West Bank for days.

Key Reforms

The protesters want an amendment of the 1994 Paris protocol, a key part of the Oslo accords that govern economic relations between Israel and the PA. Its main effect has been to keep the Palestinian economy dependent on Israel. It pegs Palestinian tax rates to Israel's much higher ones, lays open Palestinian markets to Israel, though the reverse is not true, and through various restrictions, forces the Palestinians to trade only with Israel. The resulting poverty and 40% youth unemployment have pushed people on to the streets, and they now demand the resignation of the Palestinian prime minister, Salam Fayyad, and of the PA itself. Now Abbas has proposed cancelling the whole Oslo accords, including the economic and security agreements. However, no decision was reached, and whether it's another empty threat remains to be seen.

Given this situation, should there not be a reassessment of Palestinian political strategy? To date there is no sign that the Palestinian leadership, or indeed any official body, can think beyond the two-state solution. Yet the facts on the ground point to a very different conclusion. Israel now controls 62% of West Bank land—encompassing most of its richest farmland, including the fertile Jordan Valley. The colonisation process continues unabated, and to date Israel has resisted every call for a settlement based on a two-state solution. Despite this, the west has been extremely reluctant to press Israel.

Few would dispute the Palestinian entitlement to a state, but it simply cannot be achieved given the present reality. It was always folly to pursue the two-state solution in a context that militated against its ever happening. Today's Israel-Palestine is demonstrably one state, impossible to divide. But it is a discriminatory state operating an apartheid-style system against the Palestinians with impunity. Gross economic inequality is one indicator of this system.

A New Strategy

This situation demands a new Palestinian strategy, a Plan B that converts the Palestinian struggle for two states into one for equal rights within what is now a unitary state ruled by Is-

The Israeli-Palestinian Conflict

Palestine is an area in the Middle East bounded to the west by the Mediterranean, to the north by Lebanon, to the south by the Sinai Desert, and to the east by the Jordan River. It is occupied at present by two peoples or national groups, Israelis and Arabs. Israel, a democratic republic that identifies itself as a Jewish state, was founded In 1948 and in 2008 had a population of 7.3 million (75.8 percent Jewish, 19.7 percent Arab, and 5.4 percent other). The term "Palestinians" denotes Arabs whose place of personal or recent-ancestral origin is Palestine. Some people speak of Arab Israelis as Palestinians, but the term is most often used to refer to non-Israeli Arabs in Palestine living in the major territories occupied by Israel since 1967: East Jerusalem, the West Bank of the Jordan River, and the Gaza Strip along the Mediterranean coast south of Israel. Most Palestinians are Muslim, but about 1.5 percent are Christian.

Conflict between Arabs and Jews in Palestine arose in the early twentieth century, with Arab resistance to the European Zionist project of establishing a Jewish-majority homeland in Palestine, the site of an intermittent ancient Jewish kingdom until the extension of the Roman Empire to that area in 63 BCE.

Gale Cengage Learning,
Global Issues in Context Online Collection, *2013.*

rael. The first step in this plan requires a dismantlement of the PA as currently constituted, or at least a change of direction for the Palestinian leadership. The PA's role as a buffer between the occupier and the occupied should end, along with the illusion of a spurious Palestinian autonomy it has fostered. This has not only shielded Israel from facing its legal obligations as an occupying power, but it has created a false equivalence between occupier and occupied.

The PA's new relationship with Israel should be restricted to pursuing the rights of its occupied people, including the right to political resistance. The PA should lead the campaign to prepare Palestinians for the abandonment of the two-state idea and the struggle for equal rights instead. Without a middleman to hide behind, the reality of Israel's occupation will be exposed, and the logic of a civil rights struggle will be inarguable. Israel has hitherto enjoyed a cost-free occupation, with a Palestinian leadership that does Israel's administrative and security work and a donor community that picks up the bill. At one stroke, Plan B shreds these fig leaves, and removes the chimera of a Palestinian state that has diverted attention from the reality on the ground.

The 2.5 million potential new Arab citizens of Israel would be able to challenge its much-vaunted democracy, and upend the old order in the Palestinians' favour. Will they have the courage to grasp the challenge?

> *"'Two-state condominialism' is as visionary as the name is clunky."*

Two-State Condominialism Should Be Considered as a Viable Solution

Anne-Marie Slaughter

Anne-Marie Slaughter is an author and a professor of politics and international affairs at Princeton University. In the following viewpoint, she advocates for two-state condominialism as a viable solution to the Israeli-Palestinian conflict. Slaughter contends that it offers an "eminently sensible" strategy: the creation of two states, a Palestinian state and the Jewish state of Israel; the right of Palestinians and Jews to settle anywhere in either state; and full benefits and rights for both Palestinian and Jews in either state. In essence, it would be a single, binational settlement community. This solution would recognize the inescapable interconnectedness between the Palestinian territories and Israel and would be a creative and effective way to address the issue.

As you read, consider the following questions:

1. According to Slaughter, in what year did a student named Russell Nieli present the idea of two-state condominialism?

2. Who does the author identify as the founder of the magazine *Tikkun*?

3. How many people does the author cite as members of the European Union economy?

Imagine a two-state solution in Israel and Palestine in which Palestinians would have the right of return; Israelis could settle wherever they could purchase land in the West Bank; and Jerusalem need not be divided. This is not a fanciful vision, but a creative and eminently sensible reinvention of twenty-first century statehood. And US President Barack Obama's just-completed visit to Israel provides an opportunity to explore genuinely new thinking.

The Failure of the Two-State Solution

Ever since Bill Clinton nearly succeeded in brokering a comprehensive settlement in 2000, the mantra among supporters of the Israeli-Palestinian peace process has been that, while a solution exists, Israeli and Palestinian leaders who are willing to reach it do not. The solution is a version of the deal that Clinton sought: two sovereign states based on the 1967 borders, with negotiated land swaps to reflect existing settlement patterns. The agreement would include a land corridor connecting Gaza and the West Bank; a divided Jerusalem with guaranteed access for all to religious sites; Palestinians' renunciation of the right of return; Israel's willingness to dismantle settlements outside the agreed borders; and recognition of both states across the Middle East.

But suppose that the reason that no Palestinians and Israelis willing to conclude such a deal have emerged is that the solution itself is domestically unsupportable on both sides. Suppose that as long as a version of this deal is the only game in town, the creeping physical expansion of the Israeli state and the demographic expansion of Israeli Arabs will continue to erode its foundation. For all the dire warnings that the window for a two-state solution is rapidly closing (or has already closed), it is the solution itself that is the problem.

A New Strategy

In 2008, a Princeton University graduate student in philosophy named Russell Nieli gave a talk at the Princeton Center for Jewish Life that was so well received that he later expanded it into an article for the US-based magazine *Tikkun*, founded by Rabbi Michael Lerner. The article, "Toward a Permanent Palestinian/Israeli Peace—the Case for Two-State Condominialism," was published with the express aim of stimulating "productive thinking among a younger generation of Jews and Arabs not bound by the restricted vision and failed policies of the past."

"Two-state condominialism" is as visionary as the name is clunky. The core idea is that Israelis and Palestinians would be citizens of two separate states and thus would identify with two separate political authorities. Palestine would be defined as a state of the Palestinian people, and Israel as a Jewish state. Under "condominialism," however, both Palestinians and Jews "would be granted the right to settle anywhere within the territory of either of the two states, the two states thus forming a single, binational settlement community."

Think about that for a minute. As Nieli describes it, Palestinians "would have the right to settle anywhere within Israel just as Jews would have the right to settle anywhere within the territory of the Palestinian state. Regardless of which of the two states they lived in, all Palestinians would be citizens of the Palestinian state, all Jews citizens of Israel." Each state would have the authority and the obligation to provide for the economic, cultural, religious, and welfare needs of its citizens living in the other state's territory. These would be extraterritorial rights and responsibilities, just as the United States, for example, provides for its large numbers of expatriates, such as civilian dependents of US military personnel based abroad.

To make this work, the borders of each state would first have to be defined—presumably on the basis of the 1967 borders, with mutually agreed territorial swaps. Israeli Arabs would then be required to transfer their citizenship, national identity, and national voting rights—but not their residence—to the new Palestinian state. They would have a permanent right to live in Israel and would retain the benefits to which they are currently entitled as Israeli citizens, but they would now vote as citizens of Palestine. All other Palestinians living in Israel would have rights and benefits only under Palestinian law.

Condominialism recognizes the reality of the deep interconnectedness of Israeli settlers in the West Bank with the rest of Israel—through roads, water supplies, electricity grids, administrative structures, and economic relationships (just as Israeli and Palestinian parts of Jerusalem are interdependent). Instead of trying to separate and recreate all of these structures and relationships, it makes far more sense to build on them in ways that benefit both states' peoples and economies. And, in a world in which many citizens spend an increasing proportion of their time in virtual space, *de facto* condominialism is already happening.

Rethinking Statehood

In the 1950's, after four decades of war across Europe, the idea of a European Union in which member states' citizens could live and work freely across national borders while retaining their political allegiance and cultural identity seemed equally far-fetched. (Indeed, the name of the political process by which the EU [European Union] was to be constructed, "neo-functionalism," was every bit as abstract and cumbersome as "two-state condominialism.") Yet French and German statesmen summoned the vision and the will to launch a bold experiment, one that has evolved into a single economy of 500 million people.

Why shouldn't another site of ancient enmities be the source of a new conception of statehood? Interestingly, many young people in the 1950's, like my Belgian mother, ardently supported the vision of a new Europe. Today's young Israelis and Palestinians pride themselves on their entrepreneurialism, with all the risk and vision that starting something new entails. Supporting and contributing to an innovative political start-up would be their generation's defining act.

"Irrespective of the number of states, the goal should be to dismantle those institutions that confer privilege to any particular ethnic, religious or national group."

Rethinking Israel-Palestine: Beyond Bantustans, Beyond Reservations

Noura Erakat

Noura Erakat is an activist and human rights attorney. In the following viewpoint, she notes that a just and clear-cut solution to the Israeli-Palestinian problem is out of reach; both one-state and two-state solutions have serious drawbacks and the contentious political atmosphere makes constructive political progress on the issue unattainable. Erakat argues that Israel has not approached the issue in good faith, because it is intent on preserving its political, economic, demographic, and social control over Palestinians. The vital aspect of any solution to the crisis is the dismantling of any institution that confers privilege to any particular ethnic, religious, or national group. Without that key reform, any solution will likely result in the further systematic oppression and criminalization of Palestinians.

Noura Erakat, "Rethinking Israel-Palestine: Beyond Bantustans, Beyond Reservations." Reprinted with permission from the March 21, 2013 issue of *The Nation*. For subscription information, call 1-800-333-8536. Portions of each week's Nation magazine can be accessed at http://thenation.com.

As you read, consider the following questions:

1. According to Erakat, what percentage of Israel's population did David Ben-Gurion say must be Jewish for the state to be successful?

2. What is the Law of Return, as described by the author?

3. When did apartheid end in South Africa, according to Erakat?

As President Barack Obama embarks on his listening tour in the Middle East, he is likely to witness the impact of two decades of the Oslo peace process. Twenty years, dozens of summits and millions of dollars have brought Palestinians and Israel no closer to establishing a viable peace.

The US-brokered agreement has been associated with a mantra of establishing two states for two peoples, living side by side. In fact, Israel has existed as a state since 1948 and Palestinians have remained internally displaced within that state, exiled from it and occupied by it in adjacent territories. More significantly, Jewish Israelis and non-Jewish Palestinians, Israeli citizens and stateless civilians alike, are inextricably populated throughout a single territorial entity under Israeli control. The call for two states is really a call for the separation of two populations based on ethno-national homogeneity. The proposal has failed, not just because of a lack of accountability, but because it is fundamentally flawed. Like prescribing aspirin to deal with cancer, Oslo offered truncated self-rule as a prescription for Jewish-Israeli settler-colonialism and domination.

Much like Marcus Garvey's proposition in response to the Black Question in the United States, Zionists insisted upon the creation of a Jewish homeland in response to systemic anti-Semitism in Europe. The horror of the European Holocaust catalyzed the Zionist option and has, since then, eclipsed all other responses to institutionalized and ethnic-based bigotry. It has thus been excruciatingly difficult, if not impossible, to critique Jewish-Zionist domination in Israel and the Occupied Palestinian Territory (OPT) without falling prey to accusations of anti-Semitism. Fundamentally, however, both the opposition to anti-Semitism as well as to Jewish-Israeli privilege is rooted in an anti-domination discourse.

Establishing a Demographic Majority

Due to the insistence upon maintaining a Jewish demographic majority, Israel's establishment and maintenance has necessitated the ongoing forced displacement of Muslim and Christian Palestinians. Well before Israel's establishment, David Ben-Gurion, Israel's chief architect and two-time prime minister, said that in order to be successful, Jews must comprise 80 percent of the population, hardly a plausible ratio in light of a vibrant Palestinian society in 1948. As put by the Israeli historian Benny Morris during an interview discussing his book, *The Birth of the Palestinian Refugee Problem Revisited,*

> Ben Gurion . . . understood that there could be no Jewish state with a large and hostile Arab minority in its midst . . . that has to be clear, it's impossible to evade it. Without the uprooting of the Palestinians, a Jewish state would not have arisen there.

And so based on that vision, Zionists demolished 531 Arab villages and expelled some 700,000 Palestinians from what is today Israel proper. The "problem," so to speak, is that Zionist forces did not expel *all* Palestinians. Instead, the 100,000 Palestinians remaining within Israel at the conclusion of the 1948 war today constitute a 1.2 million-person population, approximately 20 percent of Israel's total population.

Had Israel declared its borders along the 1949 armistice line, maintaining an 80 percent demographic balance may have been possible. Israel, however, has never declared any borders and, in accordance with a plan first elaborated by

Deputy Prime Minister Yigal Allon immediately after the 1967 war, it has steadily expanded into the rest of Mandate Palestine, home now to 4 million Palestinians.

As of October 2012, the balance of Jews to non-Jews throughout Israel and the OPT was approximately 5.9 million Jewish Israelis, including the settler population, and 6.1 million Palestinians.

At this juncture, Israel could abandon its commitment to a Jewish demographic majority and establish a state for all its citizens without distinction to religion. Its leaders and supporters reject this pluralistic, democratic option outright and equate it with the destruction of Israel.

Alternatively, Israel could annex the territories and impose an apartheid regime, wherein a minority rules over the majority. Israeli leaders reject this option but, notably, a significant majority of Israelis support it, as revealed by an October 2012 poll published in *Haaretz*. Although Israel refuses to formally acknowledge it, this reality currently exists as a matter of fact.

Perhaps Israel's best option for preserving a Jewish demographic majority is the establishment of a Palestinian state and the de jure establishment of international borders—the choice it abandoned more than four decades ago. Indeed, this option has received the most fervent support from the international community and the formal Palestinian leadership, represented by the Palestinian Authority, as well as Israel's most strident supporters.

Nevertheless, Israel has obliterated the two-state option since the signing of Oslo in 1993. It sanctioned, funded and encouraged, as a matter of national policy, the growth of the settler population in the West Bank, including occupied East Jerusalem, from 200,000 to nearly 600,000. It built 85 percent of the separation barrier on occupied West Bank land, circumscribing its largest settlement blocs and effectively confiscating 13 percent of the territory. Rather than prepare Area C (62 percent of the West Bank, now under interim Israeli civil and military jurisdiction) for Palestinian control, it has entrenched its settlement-colonial enterprise. Israel's siege has exacerbated the cultural, social and national distance between the Gaza Strip and the West Bank. And its intense Judaization campaign in East Jerusalem has accelerated the ethnic cleansing of Palestinians there, hardly preparing it to become the independent capital of the future Palestinian state.

For liberal Zionists who believe that the preservation of Israel as a Jewish state and the protection of Palestinian dignity and freedom are compatible, this predicament is especially curious—why would Israel sabotage its best available option? Crudely put, because Israel's preferred option is the one that it has always pursued: the establishment of absolute control over Palestinians as a fragmented and dispensable underclass, without distinction to their status as citizens of Israel or civilians under occupation.

Zionists did not historically conceive of Palestinians as a national polity entitled to self-determination; they were not considered a "people" at all. Palestinian self-representation, resistance and international recognition, however, have forced even the most ardent Zionists to reconsider this proposition. Notwithstanding their accepted standing as a people today, Israel continues to deal with Mandate Palestine's non-Jewish indigenous population as a demographic, national and cultural impediment to its settler-colonial project rather than a constituent or future neighbor.

Ethno-National Domination

Upon its establishment, Israel passed a series of laws that privileged its Jewish inhabitants and further dispossessed and marginalized its non-Jewish indigenous population. Two laws are particularly relevant: the Citizenship Law (1952) bifurcated Jewish nationality from Israeli citizenship and denationalized the Palestinian population. In doing so, the state instantly created a two-tiered system of rights: one available for

South African Apartheid

Apartheid was the official government policy in South Africa from 1948 to 1994. During that time, the white South African government passed a number of laws that deprived blacks, coloureds (people of mixed ancestry), and Asians of basic rights—taking away their property and political rights and restricting their movement and activities. Many black South Africans were moved to reserves called homelands, where they were expected to develop their own self-governing societies. But the homelands consisted of poor quality lands with insufficient resources, and residents lived in extreme poverty.

Gale Cengage Learning,
Global Issues in Context Online Collection, *2013.*

Jews, who could be both nationals and citizens, and one for non-Jews, who could be citizens only. The Law of Return (1950) extended the right to Israeli citizenship and associated state benefits to any Jewish person, now a Jewish national as well, anywhere in the world.

Together these laws ensured that Jewish persons who lived beyond Israel's boundaries and had no relationship to it had more rights than the state's own non-Jewish Palestinian citizens, even when their meager numbers did not constitute one-fifth of Israel's population, as they do today. Not only was a nascent Israel cementing its Jewish demographic majority, but by instituting a series of similar laws, it also preserved Jewish political, social and economic privilege.

Notwithstanding the significant demographic majority of Jews to non-Jews within Israel proper, Israel has treated its Palestinian citizens as a fifth column. The State Department's 2005 Annual Human Rights Report notes that there is institutionalized legal and societal discrimination against Israel's Christian, Muslim and Druze citizens. The government does not provide Israeli Arabs with the same quality of education, housing, employment and social services as Jews.

In addition to their socioeconomic subjugation, Israel has also worked to thwart the national identity of, and social solidarity among, its minority and indigenous Palestinian population.

In furtherance of its demographic priorities, some of these Israeli policies have had the express purpose of reducing the size of its Palestinian population. The Nationality and Entry into Israel Law (Temporary Order), better known as the Ban on Family Reunification, for example, prohibits the adjustment of status and acquisition of citizenship among spouses from the Occupied Palestinian Territory and "enemy states," not coincidentally all the states with a high concentration of Palestinians: Lebanon, Syria, Iran and Iraq. In its January 2012 decision upholding the law, the Israeli High Court of Justice explained, "human rights are not a prescription for national suicide."

But the threat is not just numeric; it is just as much about competing narratives and memory. At stake is the state's own national mythology.

In 2011, Israel passed the State Budget Law Amendment. Popularly known as the Nakba Law, it penalizes, by revoking state funding, any institution that either challenges Israel's founding as a Jewish and democratic state or commemorates Israel's Independence Day as one of mourning or loss. The threat any such commemoration poses is a challenge to Israel's narrative of righteous conception.

The Prawer Plan, named after its author, former deputy chair of the National Security Council Ehud Prawer, seeks to forcibly displace up to 70,000 Palestinian Bedouins from their homes and communities in the Negev Desert to urban townships to make room for Jewish-only settlements and a forest. The plan, approved in September 2011, has no demographic impact, as these Palestinians are already Israeli citizens. It does, however, violently sever these Bedouin communities from their agricultural livelihoods and centuries-long association with that particular land.

Similarly, in 2001 the High Court of Justice rejected an appeal from internally displaced Palestinians to return to the villages of Ikrit and Kafr Bir'im, near the Lebanon border, from which they were forcibly displaced in 1948. Like the Negev-based Palestinians, these Palestinians are Israeli citizens and therefore pose no demographic threat. In fact, they currently live only miles away from their demolished villages. Their return to them only threatens a Zionist narrative that Palestine was a land without a people for a people without a land. To further the erasure, Israel plans on building Jewish settlements where these communities once lived.

Israel's land and housing planning policies in the Galilee demonstrate that the threat is not just about demographics and memory but the cohesion of Palestinians within the state, and the potential for Palestinian nationalism. In Nazareth, home to 80,000 Palestinian citizens of Israel, bidding rights for public building opportunities are reserved for citizens who have completed military service. This excludes nearly all of Nazareth's Palestinian population, who do not serve in the Israeli military for historical and political reasons. In other Galilee cities, "Admissions Committees" can legally exclude Palestinians from their residential communities for being "socially unsuitable" based on their race or national origin alone. Together with its policy of Jewish settlement expansion *within* Israel as well as a matrix of similarly discriminatory urban planning laws, Israel forces its Palestinian citizens to live in noncontiguous ghettos throughout the state.

Palestinian refugees fundamentally disrupt these national goals: their return would shatter Israel's Jewish majority, their presence is a living testament of Palestinian narrative and memory, and their historical claims dislocate the ghettoization of Palestinians within Israel today. The absence of refugees, however, does not reverse Israel's policies aimed at diminishing the number of Palestinians, concentrating them geographically and separating them from one another.

Abandoning the right of return for refugees in this context is therefore not "pragmatic" at all. Refugees are not the impediment to establishing a viable peace; its most formidable impediment is Israel's insistence upon Jewish primacy throughout Israel and the OPT.

Inadequate Remedies

A Palestinian state is hardly adequate to remedy these conditions. At best, it responds to Israel's hegemonic ambitions by establishing an Arab Muslim and Christian corollary where Palestinians can assert their own ethno-national dominance. It disregards the broader Palestinian question, which stems from their forced displacement, exile and occupation. In contrast to the international enthusiasm today for a Palestinian state, in 1976 the UN General Assembly, in response to the establishment of Transkei, a self-governing authority within the South African Republic, passed Resolution 31/6 A, which condemned

> the establishment of bantustans as designed to consolidate the inhuman policies of *apartheid*, to destroy the territorial integrity of the country, to perpetuate white minority domination and to dispossess the African people of South Africa of their inalienable rights.

Even a single democratic, secular state without a concomitant anti-domination movement will not suffice to remedy these conditions. Irrespective of the number of states, the goal should be to dismantle those institutions that confer privilege to any particular ethnic, religious or national group. As indicated by the outstanding poverty gaps between blacks and whites in South Africa after the nominal end of apartheid in the early 1990s, this must include more than a simple removal of discriminatory laws. Transitional justice must feature rehabilitative policies as well. Equality under the law alone will do little to alleviate the criminalization of minority, indigenous communities, as indicated in the United States by the striking proportion of incarcerated Native Americans in the states where their numbers are still significant. To adequately remedy institutionalized discrimination and subjugation, reformed state institutions should also be imbued with an ethos of socioeconomic dignity for all its citizens and residents.

Failure to do so in Israel and the OPT will likely result in the de facto ghettoization, systematic impoverishment and criminalization of Palestinians regardless of their pre-existing status as citizens, civilians or refugees. Under such circumstances, in a one-state solution, their condition would be like Native American reservations, and in a two-state solution, they will be like South African bantustans. Both ought to be rejected in favor of a democratic and dignified one-state formula as only the first step.

| *"The borders of Israel and Palestine should be based on the 1967 lines."*

A Palestinian State Should Be Based on Pre-1967 Borders

Barack Obama

Barack Obama is the forty-fourth president of the United States. In the following viewpoint, he underscores the need for a lasting peace in the Middle East and views the implementation of a two-state solution for Israel and the Palestinian people as key for that goal. Obama proposes that the creation of a Palestinian state should be based on pre-1967 borders with mutually agreed swaps. By at least using these borders as a basis of negotiations, Israelis and Palestinians should be able to come to an agreement that respects the rights of both parties. Although the peace process will be very difficult, it is vital to the future of the region, he maintains. He asserts that much of the Middle East is facing some of the same challenges—confronting political oppression and economic inequality—and only by addressing these issues will there be a more peaceful and stable world.

As you read, consider the following questions:

1. According to Obama, what two emotional issues will remain once Israel and Palestine agree on permanent borders?

Barack Obama, "Remarks by the President on the Middle East and North Africa," www .whitehouse.gov, May 19, 2011.

2. What question does the Fatah-Hamas reconciliation hold for Israel, according to the author?

3. What belief does Obama say the United States was founded on?

For decades, the conflict between Israelis and Arabs has cast a shadow over the [Mideast] region. For Israelis, it has meant living with the fear that their children could be blown up on a bus or by rockets fired at their homes, as well as the pain of knowing that other children in the region are taught to hate them. For Palestinians, it has meant suffering the humiliation of occupation, and never living in a nation of their own. Moreover, this conflict has come with a larger cost to the Middle East, as it impedes partnerships that could bring greater security and prosperity and empowerment to ordinary people.

The Prospects of a Lasting Peace

For over two years, my administration has worked with the parties and the international community to end this conflict, building on decades of work by previous administrations. Yet expectations have gone unmet. Israeli settlement activity [in the Palestinian territories] continues. Palestinians have walked away from talks. The world looks at a conflict that has grinded on and on and on, and sees nothing but stalemate. Indeed, there are those who argue that with all the change and uncertainty in the region, it is simply not possible to move forward now.

I disagree. At a time when the people of the Middle East and North Africa are casting off the burdens of the past [the so-called Arab Spring], the drive for a lasting peace that ends the conflict and resolves all claims is more urgent than ever. That's certainly true for the two parties involved.

For the Palestinians, efforts to delegitimize Israel will end in failure. Symbolic actions to isolate Israel at the United Nations in September won't create an independent state. Palestinian leaders will not achieve peace or prosperity if [militant Islamist party] Hamas insists on a path of terror and rejection. And Palestinians will never realize their independence by denying the right of Israel to exist.

As for Israel, our friendship is rooted deeply in a shared history and shared values. Our commitment to Israel's security is unshakeable. And we will stand against attempts to single it out for criticism in international forums. But precisely because of our friendship, it's important that we tell the truth: The status quo is unsustainable, and Israel too must act boldly to advance a lasting peace.

The fact is, a growing number of Palestinians live west of the Jordan River. Technology will make it harder for Israel to defend itself. A region undergoing profound change will lead to populism in which millions of people—not just one or two leaders—must believe peace is possible. The international community is tired of an endless process that never produces an outcome. The dream of a Jewish and democratic state cannot be fulfilled with permanent occupation.

A Two-State Solution

Now, ultimately, it is up to the Israelis and Palestinians to take action. No peace can be imposed upon them—not by the United States; not by anybody else. But endless delay won't make the problem go away. What America and the international community can do is to state frankly what everyone knows—a lasting peace will involve two states for two peoples: Israel as a Jewish state and the homeland for the Jewish people, and the state of Palestine as the homeland for the Palestinian people, each state enjoying self-determination, mutual recognition, and peace.

So while the core issues of the conflict must be negotiated, the basis of those negotiations is clear: a viable Palestine, a secure Israel. The United States believes that negotiations should result in two states, with permanent Palestinian borders with Israel, Jordan, and Egypt, and permanent Israeli borders with Palestine. We believe the borders of Israel and Palestine should be based on the 1967 lines with mutually agreed swaps, so that secure and recognized borders are established for both states. The Palestinian people must have the right to govern themselves, and reach their full potential, in a sovereign and contiguous state.

As for security, every state has the right to self-defense, and Israel must be able to defend itself—by itself—against any threat. Provisions must also be robust enough to prevent a resurgence of terrorism, to stop the infiltration of weapons, and to provide effective border security. The full and phased withdrawal of Israeli military forces should be coordinated with the assumption of Palestinian security responsibility in a sovereign, non-militarized state. And the duration of this transition period must be agreed [on], and the effectiveness of security arrangements must be demonstrated.

These principles provide a foundation for negotiations. Palestinians should know the territorial outlines of their state; Israelis should know that their basic security concerns will be met. I'm aware that these steps alone will not resolve the conflict, because two wrenching and emotional issues will remain: the future of Jerusalem, and the fate of Palestinian refugees. But moving forward now on the basis of territory and security provides a foundation to resolve those two issues in a way that is just and fair, and that respects the rights and aspirations of both Israelis and Palestinians.

Difficult Negotiations

Now, let me say this: Recognizing that negotiations need to begin with the issues of territory and security does not mean that it will be easy to come back to the table. In particular, the recent announcement of an agreement between [political party] Fatah and Hamas raises profound and legitimate ques-

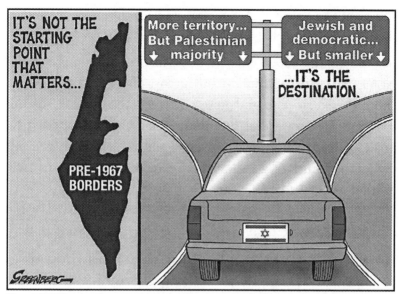

"Israel 1967 Borders," cartoon by Steve Greenberg. Copyright © by Steve Greenberg. Reproduction rights obtainable from www.CartoonStock.com.

tions for Israel: How can one negotiate with a party that has shown itself unwilling to recognize your right to exist? And in the weeks and months to come, Palestinian leaders will have to provide a credible answer to that question. Meanwhile, the United States, our Quartet partners [namely, the UN, European Union, and Russia], and the Arab states will need to continue every effort to get beyond the current impasse.

I recognize how hard this will be. Suspicion and hostility has been passed on for generations, and at times it has hardened. But I'm convinced that the majority of Israelis and Palestinians would rather look to the future than be trapped in the past. We see that spirit in the Israeli father whose son was killed by Hamas, who helped start an organization that brought together Israelis and Palestinians who had lost loved ones. That father said, "I gradually realized that the only hope for progress was to recognize the face of the conflict." We see it in the actions of a Palestinian who lost three daughters to Israeli shells in Gaza. "I have the right to feel angry," he said.

"So many people were expecting me to hate. My answer to them is I shall not hate. Let us hope," he said, "for tomorrow."

That is the choice that must be made—not simply in the Israeli-Palestinian conflict, but across the entire region—a choice between hate and hope; between the shackles of the past and the promise of the future. It's a choice that must be made by leaders and by the people, and it's a choice that will define the future of a region that served as the cradle of civilization and a crucible of strife.

The Challenges Ahead

For all the challenges that lie ahead, we see many reasons to be hopeful. In Egypt, we see it in the efforts of young people who led protests. In Syria, we see it in the courage of those who brave bullets while chanting, "peaceful, peaceful." In Benghazi, a city threatened with destruction, we see it in the courthouse square where people gather to celebrate the freedoms that they had never known. Across the region, those rights that we take for granted are being claimed with joy by those who are prying lose the grip of an iron fist.

For the American people, the scenes of upheaval in the region may be unsettling, but the forces driving it are not unfamiliar. Our own nation was founded through a rebellion against an empire. Our people fought a painful Civil War that extended freedom and dignity to those who were enslaved. And I would not be standing here today unless past generations turned to the moral force of nonviolence as a way to perfect our union—organizing, marching, protesting peacefully together to make real those words that declared our nation: "We hold these truths to be self-evident, that all men are created equal."

Those words must guide our response to the change that is transforming the Middle East and North Africa—words which tell us that repression will fail, and that tyrants will fall, and that every man and woman is endowed with certain in-alienable rights.

It will not be easy. There's no straight line to progress, and hardship always accompanies a season of hope. But the United States of America was founded on the belief that people should govern themselves. And now we cannot hesitate to stand squarely on the side of those who are reaching for their rights, knowing that their success will bring about a world that is more peaceful, more stable, and more just.

> *"It seems clear that demanding that ne-gotiations start from Israel's pre-1967 borders will not bring peace."*

Return Israel to pre-1967 Borders? How About Returning the US to 1844 (or 1802 or 1861) Borders?

George Berkin

George Berkin is a reporter and political commentator. In the following viewpoint, he rejects Barack Obama's proposal that Is-rael should accept the pre-1967 borders as a starting point for negotiations with the Palestinians. Berkin suggests that reverting to those borders would compromise Israel's national security and violate its right to occupy its historical territory. In addition, there is no reason that Israel should compromise with Palestin-ian officials who have denied Israel's right to exist—and in some cases, have been deemed terrorist organizations. Most impor-tantly, such a momentous concession would not resolve the con-flict and would, in fact, encourage the Palestinians to demand the total annihilation of Israel.

George Berkin, "Return Israel to pre-1967 Borders? How About Returning the US to 1844 (or 1802 or 1861) Borders?," *NJ Voices*, May 25, 2011. Reproduced with permission.

As you read, consider the following questions:

1. During what war did Israel take control of east Jerusalem, the West Bank, Gaza, and the Golan Heights, according to the author?

2. What US state does Berkin compare to Israel's current size?

3. According to Berkin, returning to pre-1967 borders would require Israel to hand over part of what key city?

How's this prescription for solving our conflict (illegal immigrants and drugs) with Mexico: *Renegotiate the border,* starting with where the line stood in *1844* (i.e. before we acquired a large chunk of territory in the Mexican War).

Or here's a suggestion for resolving problems between Washington and Paris: renegotiate the western U.S. border based on geographic lines in effect in *1802,* before the Louisiana Purchase.

While we're at it, let's return to the geography of *July 1861,* just after the Confederate states declared their independence but before the Civil War set things back to right.

Hey, why not? *Overturning established borders* to return to a previous line of demarcation sounds like a good idea, especially for those unhappy with the status quo.

If you agree with that line of argument, you are probably applauding the proposal set forth by President *Barack Obama* at the State Department last week. In his speech, President Obama advocated that Israel accept the "pre-1967" borders as a starting point for negotiations with the Palestinians.

The proposal would give to the Palestinians the land won by Israel in the Six-Day War of June 1967, including east Jerusalem, the West Bank, Gaza and the Golan Heights. As a so-called "concession," Israel could keep land settled by Israeli residents since then, but only if Israel gave up equivalent parcels of land in other parts of pre-1967 Israel.

Not surprisingly, Israeli Prime Minister *Benjamin Netanyahu* rebuked President Obama the day after the president's speech, the Israeli leader rightly reminding him that reverting to the pre-1967 borders would make it nearly impossible for Israel to defend itself. Israel is now roughly the size of New Jersey, but adopting the pre-1967 borders would return Israel to being just nine miles wide along its northern "neck."

And on Tuesday, Netanyahu *told* a joint session of the U.S. Congress that Jerusalem must remain undivided and all of the city must belong to Israel. The Israeli prime minister also told members of Congress that *Judea* and *Samaria*—the biblical names for the West Bank—were historically part of the ancient Jewish homeland.

I might remind readers that what is now called the West Bank was part of Israel more than 3,000 years ago. The Romans, who arrived much later, called the territory *Palestine*, "land of the Philistines." The new occupiers named the territory after the enemies of Israel, as a poke in the eye to the Jews.

In making his proposal, President Obama has been more than a little disingenuous. During his speech last week, President Obama characterized his proposal as a bold new step to jump-start the peace process. (Bold, yes, because President Obama abandoned all pretence at even-handedness and threw the weight of U.S. prestige onto the Palestinian side of the conflict.)

After a firestorm erupted, President Obama backtracked, claiming that he was merely restating a long-standing U.S. position. That is nonsense; there was a reason why the President's speech was not ignored as simply nothing new.

There was also more than a little attempted intimidation in President Obama's proposal. Palestinian leaders have threatened to officially "declare" Palestinian statehood in September, and bring it to a vote before the United Nations, unless there

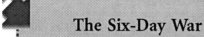

The Six-Day War

In 1947, the United Nations (UN) Special Committee on Palestine proposed a partition of Palestine into two states, one majority Arab and the other majority Jewish. The proposal sparked a war between Jewish and Arab forces. Zionist forces declared Israel's independence on 14 May 1948. The new state was immediately attacked by Egypt and Jordan, two neighboring Arab states. During the violence in the region, over 700 thousand Palestinian Arab civilians fled the territory that is now Israel, fearing attacks by Israeli forces.

When the war ended with a U.N.-brokered ceasefire in 1949, Israel had held its claimed territory and Jordan had occupied what is now known as the West Bank, an area on Israel's western flank. Gaza, a coastal area south of Israel, declared itself an independent Palestinian state with its capital in Jerusalem (not located in Gaza, but symbolically important to Christians and Muslims). . . . In 1967, another war broke out and Israel occupied Gaza, East Jerusalem, the Golan Heights, and the West Bank. Today, these areas are termed the Occupied Territories in international discourse: for example, the UN speaks of "the Occupied Territories" or "Occupied Palestinian Territory" in its documents. The term is not accepted by Israel, which considers the territories "disputed," not "occupied."

Today, the word "Palestinians" is most often used to refer to Arabs living in the Occupied Territories, where they are the majority of the population. As of 2008, there were about 3.7 million Palestinians living in the Occupied Territories. Another 7 million or so Palestinians lived as expatriates, citizens, or refugees in a number of other countries, notably Israel (1.3 million) and Jordan (2.7 million).

Gale Cengage Learning,
Global Issues in Context Online, *2013.*

is "progress" in talks between the Israelis and the Palestinians. In other words, hand over territory—or else!

President Obama's speech also follows the recent reconciliation between *Hamas*, which runs Gaza, and *Fatah*, by which the *Palestinian Authority* exercises a measure of control in the West Bank. However, Hamas denies Israel's right to exist. Hama also has never renounced terror as a political strategy. The U.S., not surprisingly, identifies Hamas as a terrorist organization.

In other words, two Palestinian organizations—including a self-proclaimed terrorist group opposed to Israel's existence—have teamed up to redefine Israel's borders.

My *opening examples of American territorial revisionism are ridiculous, of course. The U.S. would never agree to go back to previous borders*, no matter how much other parties might promise that doing so would bring peace to the Southwest or improve relations with France or South Carolina.

But the analogy breaks down for other reasons—instructive reasons as we think about how the Palestinians are determined to destroy Israel.

First, none of the examples at the beginning of this post asks the U.S. to surrender part of Washington, D.C., the political (and emotional) seat of our government. But the "pre-1967" borders that President Obama wants Israel to return to would require the Jewish state to hand over part of Jerusalem, the political, emotional and spiritual *heart of Israel*.

Second, Americans would certainly feel bad about handing over part of the Southwest to Mexico. But no one can credibly claim that doing so would make it nearly *impossible to defend* what remained of our nation.

Not so were Israel to give up the territories it won—in a defensive war—against its assembled enemies nearly a half-century ago. Some commentators have pointed to Israel's success in defending itself in 1967 as "proof" that Israel could repeat that military success, if worse came to worse. But having succeeded once before, under remarkable circumstances, is not a solid security strategy.

Third, none of my examples of territorial "givebacks" would be a first step to an ultimate *goal of destroying* the United States. Again, we would regret losing Texas and part of California, but the U.S. would remain standing. Mexico accepts the U.S.'s right to exist.

Interestingly, President Obama's proposed return to the pre-1967 borders does not even suggest that such an enormous concession by the Israelis would end the conflict. He cast the proposal as a starting point for negotiations—*even before* Palestinians have a change of heart and agree, without mental reservations, that Israel has every right to exist in its own land.

Over the decades, the Israelis have made many concessions, all in desperate attempts to conciliate their irreconcilable neighbors. In the Camp David Accords, Egypt obtained the Sinai Peninsula in exchange for peace. The peace has lasted for several decades, but may now be imperiled by a change in political leadership in Egypt.

Yasser Arafat was offered nearly all he demanded, but he rejected Israeli concessions to continue his war against Israel. As recently as 2005, the Israelis handed over control of Gaza to Hamas, the terrorist group. Peace has not resulted. And just last week, shortly before the Obama bombshell, Netanyahu outlined to the Knesset possible concessions to a future Palestinian state.

It seems clear that demanding that negotiations start from Israel's pre-1967 borders will not bring peace. Instead, *Palestinian leaders,* flush with a "pre-1967" victory, would establish a Palestinian state, and then make their next demand. They *would demand a return to the area's pre-1948 borders—that is, a return to the days before Israel became a new nation.*

Periodical and Internet Sources Bibliography

The following articles have been selected to supplement the diverse views presented in this chapter.

Kenneth Bandler	"The Two State Solution Requires Vision, Courage, Determination," *Jerusalem Post* (Israel), August 5, 2013.
Alon Ben-Meir	"Two States for Two People," *Huffington Post*, August 16, 2011. www.huffingtonpost.com.
Jonathan Kuttab	"Steps to Create an Israel-Palestine," *Los Angeles Times*, December 20, 2009.
Ian S. Lustick	"Two-State Illusion," *New York Times*, September 14, 2013.
Saree Makdisi	"If Not Two States, Then One," *New York Times*, December 5, 2012.
Noah Millman	"The One-State Illusion," *American Conservative*, December 11, 2012.
M.J. Rosenberg	"Israel-Palestine: The One-State Solution Is a Fantasy," *Huffington Post*, January 28, 2013. www.huffingtonpost.com.
Jake Wallis Simons	"It's Sad, but a One-State Solution in Israel Will Never Work," *Daily Telegraph* (London), April 29, 2013.
William Sullivan	"Why Israel Cannot Accept Palestinian Conditions," *FrontPage Magazine*, January 5, 2012.
Ben White	"Israel and Palestine: Two States, Two Peoples," Al Jazeera, May 4, 2012. http://america.aljazeera.com.

OPPOSING
VIEWPOINTS®
SERIES

CHAPTER 2

Should the United Nations Grant Palestinian Statehood?

Chapter Preface

On November 29, 2012, the United Nations General Assembly voted to grant Palestine nonmember observer status in the United Nations. The final vote was 138–9, with Canada, Israel, and the United States three of the dissenting votes. It was a symbolic victory for the Palestinians, who were rejected for full membership status at the United Nations in 2011. The lopsided vote was considered an affirmation of Palestine's legitimacy and signaled overwhelming international support for the effort to establish an independent Palestinian state in the Middle East. However, Palestinian officials admit that it will do little to make a difference in the lives of suffering Palestinian people and might put additional obstacles in the path of a lasting peace agreement between Israel and the Palestinians.

Nonmember observer status in the United Nations may be symbolic, but commentators note that it also provides some benefits. Palestinian representatives will be allowed to speak at United Nations General Assembly meetings, participate in debates, sponsor resolutions, and take part in procedural votes. However, they will not be allowed to vote on resolutions.

For Palestinian officials, the United Nations vote provided legitimacy and a renewed opportunity to establish a sovereign Palestinian state. In his speech before the United Nations, Palestinian Authority president Mahmoud Abbas expressed the hope that Israel and Palestine could come together to implement a two-state solution and forge a lasting peace in the region. "We did not come here to delegitimize a State established years ago, and that is Israel; rather we came here to affirm the legitimacy of the State that must now achieve its independence, and that is Palestine," Abbas stated. "We did not come here to add further complications to the peace process, which Israel's policies have thrown into the intensive care unit; rather we came to launch a final serious attempt to achieve peace. Our endeavor is not aimed at terminating what remains of the negotiations process, which has lost its objective and credibility, but rather aimed at trying to breathe new life into the negotiations and at setting a solid foundation for it based on the terms of reference of the relevant international resolutions in order for the negotiations to succeed."

In her speech to the General Assembly explaining the US vote on the resolution, Susan Rice, the US permanent representative to the United Nations, also touched on the need for renewed negotiations between Israel and the Palestinians. "The backers of today's resolution say they seek a functioning, independent Palestinian state at peace with Israel," Rice said. "So do we. But we have long been clear that the only way to establish such a Palestinian state and resolve all permanent-status issues is through the crucial, if painful, work of direct negotiations between the parties. . . . Today's grand pronouncements will soon fade. And the Palestinian people will wake up tomorrow and find that little about their lives has changed, save that the prospects of a durable peace have only receded."

The implications of Palestinian statehood in the United Nations are considered in the following chapter. Viewpoints included in the section discuss the impact of the abovementioned vote on the Middle East peace process, its symbolic value to the Palestinian people and the international community, and whether the vote has exposed Israel's contradictory policy toward the Palestinians.

"There is no such thing as a Palestinian state, and the United Nations can't conjure one into existence."

No to the Palestinian "State"

National Review

The National Review *is a conservative news and political affairs magazine. In the following viewpoint, its editors urge the United States to veto the Palestinian statehood effort at the United Nations. The editors argue that there is no such thing as a Palestinian state: under international law, there are specific criteria that define the existence of a state—and Palestine does not meet any of them. Granting Palestinian statehood would isolate Israel in the international community and make the Israeli government subject to international legal proceedings, the authors contend. It may also inspire more violence and further complicate peace negotiations between Israel and the Palestinian Authority. The US government has encouraged Palestinian efforts to gain statehood and is therefore responsible for the consequences, the* National Review *concludes.*

As you read, consider the following questions:

1. How does the *National Review* describe the Montevideo Convention of 1933?

"No to the Palestinian 'State,'" *National Review*, September 19, 2011. Reproduced with permission.

2. What do the authors view as the main danger of granting Palestinian statehood?

3. According to the *National Review*, why is the reemergence of Turkey as a regional power ominous?

There is no such thing as a Palestinian state, and the United Nations can't conjure one into existence. That apparently won't stop the Palestinians from seeking recognition as a state in the Security Council this week. We should veto the Palestinian effort without hesitation.

On top of its legal nullity, the push for recognition at the U.N. trashes the spirit of the Oslo Accords, which commit both the Israelis and the Palestinians to addressing their differences through negotiations. Thwarted at the Security Council, the Palestinians will likely go to the rabble in the General Assembly, where we don't have a veto and they will presumably succeed in putting a fig leaf on a fraud.

The General Assembly can change the status of the PLO from an observer "entity," as it is now, to a "non-member state" observer, like the Vatican, and thereby recognize it indirectly as a state. But this won't create a real state, either in law or in fact. Under international law, the Montevideo Convention of 1933 explicitly provides that the existence of a sovereign state is independent of recognition by other states, and further provides that a state must have a permanent population, a defined territory, a government, and the capacity to enter into relations with other states. The Palestinians arguably have none of those things. By their own admission, they don't have a defined territory. Their government, meanwhile, is riven: Terrorists control one half of the territories and the other half is controlled by a former terrorist whose term of office expired two years ago.

Nobody would like to see the Palestinians under a functioning state of laws more than the Israelis. But a state must have a monopoly of violence, and Hamas has always rejected

The Flotilla Incident

On 31 May 2010, a flotilla of six vessels carrying humanitarian aid and activists bound for the blockaded Gaza Strip was raided by Israeli commandos. Nine of the passengers aboard the *Mavi Marmara*, a Turkish-flagged vessel that was part of the flotilla attempting to break through the blockade of Gaza, were killed, prompting worldwide condemnation and widespread protests in Turkey. Gaza has been blockaded by Israel since 2007, when the anti-Israel terrorist and political group Hamas ousted the Fatah leaders in a violent coup and took control of Gaza. But as a humanitarian crisis in the blockaded territory developed and worsened, international opinion began to shift against Israel and in favor of the Palestinians, whom many view as victims of Israeli aggression.

The deadly 31 May Israeli raid on the Gaza aid flotilla further strained already tense relations between the United States and Israel. The United States found itself in the difficult position of having to "choose sides" between key allies Israel and Turkey.

Gale Cengage Learning, Global Issues in Context, *2013.*

the monopoly of violence in favor of the inherent individual right of resistance to occupation. The Palestinians have barely managed to maintain political institutions of any kind, and a declaration of statehood will do nothing to solve that problem.

Any action in the cause of Palestinian statehood at the U.N. will serve to isolate Israel further, and could make its government subject to international legal proceedings. But the main danger is the effect it could have in the Muslim world, including the occupied territories. Another intifada would force Israel to resort to military measures, giving Egypt and Turkey another excuse to express their growing hostility to the Jewish state.

The Middle East has come to this pass despite President Obama's blithe belief at the inception of his administration that he could forge an Israeli-Palestinian peace. From the start, Obama cast his role in the Middle East as one of impartial mediator, not realizing that America's influence among the Palestinians requires Israel's confidence that we will protect the Jewish state come what may. Anyone can play the role of mediator, but only America can underwrite the risks of a negotiated settlement for both sides. The strategic prerequisites for Israeli-Palestinian peace are the same as they were for peace between Israel and Egypt in the 1970s: We must convince the Arabs that they can get what they want from the Israelis only by going through us, and we can deliver Israeli concessions only if we can guarantee Israel's security.

Yet the Obama administration has reprised the Clinton administration's childish schoolyard spats with Israeli prime minister Bibi Netanyahu. By embracing the Palestinian insistence on a halt to settlement construction as a precondition for talks, Obama encouraged the Palestinians to dig in their heels. Now the Palestinians think they can get what they want by forcing the issue at the U.N. and encouraging Egyptian and Turkish belligerence.

The new government of Egypt is seeking legitimacy by embracing the worst anti-Israeli sentiments of its populace. The army recently stood by as a Cairo mob ransacked the Israeli embassy. The Camp David Accords of 1979 are starting to crumble. Because no combination of Arab states could afford to go to war with Israel without Egypt's help, Henry Kissinger realized that peace between Israel and Egypt would end the era of Arab-Israeli wars. The fraying of the Camp David Accords, which preserved a tenuous peace for more than three decades, is ominous. So is the reemergence of Turkey as a regional power. Turkey has pledged a military escort for the next "humanitarian flotilla" aimed at forcibly breaching the Gaza blockade, a fully legal blockade even according to the United Nations.

The Middle East is again on the cusp of crisis, with the U.N. about to stoke the flames and the Obama administration caught in a self-imposed impotence.

> *"After years of presenting itself as the reasonable party in the conflict . . . [Israel elects] a slate of candidates dominated by hard-line rightists who oppose Israeli-Palestinian compromise and reject Palestinian statehood."*

Statehood Exposes Israel's Contradictory Palestinian Policy

J.J. Goldberg

J.J. Goldberg is an author, syndicated columnist, reporter, and editor at large of the Jewish Daily Forward, *a New York City newspaper. In the following viewpoint, he suggests that the controversy surrounding the issue of Palestinian statehood at the United Nations has revealed Israel's opposition to the very idea of Palestinian independence. Goldberg asserts that after years of portraying itself as a reasonable and willing partner in peace negotiations, it has become quite clear that Israel has embraced intransigence and injustice. A major part of Israel's intractable position is the election of hard-right politicians who are intent on keeping the Palestinians powerless. Another problem is the con-*

J. J. Goldberg, "Who Stands Against Peace?," *The Jewish Daily Forward*, November 29, 2012. Reproduced with permission.

tradictory strategy of Israeli prime minister Benjamin Netan-yahu, who speaks out of both sides of his mouth when it comes to the two-state solution and the peace process, Goldberg asserts.

As you read, consider the following questions:

1. According to Goldberg, when did the Palestine Liberation Organization formally ask the United Nations to recognize Palestine as a nonmember state?

2. How many countries does the author say have their embassies in greater Tel Aviv?

3. When did Benjamin Netanyahu embrace the two-state solution, according to the author?

The last days of November 2012 were an awkward time for Israel in the international arena. After years of presenting itself as the reasonable party in the conflict, saddled with a Palestinian negotiating partner that won't negotiate, its ruling Likud party wound up a two-day Knesset [Israel's parliament] primary vote on November 26 by choosing a slate of candidates dominated by hard-line rightists who oppose Israeli-Palestinian compromise and reject Palestinian statehood.

The next day, Tuesday the 27th, the Palestine Liberation Organization [PLO] formally asked the United Nations to recognize Palestine as a non-member state "living side by side in peace and security with Israel." As expected, the proposed state would be set up "on the basis of the pre-1967 borders, with delineation of final borders to be determined in final status negotiations." The negotiations would let Israel seek border adjustments to protect its airport and preserve its main settlement blocs.

Poor Timing

The timing of the two events could hardly be worse from Israel's point of view. Israel objects to the very idea of the Palestinians asking the United Nations to grant them statehood.

According to the 1993 Oslo Accords, Palestine's ultimate status is to be decided in direct negotiations between them, not by an outside party.

Israeli spokesmen say the Palestinian U.N. gambit is a violation of the 1993 accords. This sounds a bit rich coming from people who've spent the last 19 years denouncing the accords as an Israeli "suicide pact," but that's politics for you.

More to the point, defining the contours of the Palestinian state "on the basis of the pre-1967 borders" is a poison pill, at least to Israel's prime minister, Benjamin Netanyahu. In his view, this pre-empts the biggest question before talks even begin, leaving only details to be negotiated. Netanyahu insists negotiations commence without such preconditions. The Palestinians' U.N. bid looks like an end run. It lets them come to the table on his terms while the world body watches and keeps score.

However you slice it, the events make for terrible Israeli P.R [public relations]. Just when the Palestinians are putting their best face forward, asking for international certification of their desire to live peacefully alongside Israel, Israel's political system adopts a blueprint for a government after the January elections that seemingly has nothing to offer the Palestinians but the back of a fist.

The Jerusalem Issue

Further complicating Israel's position, the PLO resolution calls "for a way to be found through negotiations to resolve the status of Jerusalem as the capital of two states." That should be music to Israeli ears. It's the first formal international recognition of Jerusalem as Israel's capital, at least since the handful of embassies once located there decamped for Tel Aviv in the early 1980s. If the holy city's status were resolved, it would clear the path for America and the other 85 countries with embassies in greater Tel Aviv to end the insult and move their offices to the capital. That is, if Israel were willing to play ball and allow a Palestinian capital in the city's eastern half.

That was hard to imagine before the Likud primaries. The complexion of the party's next Knesset faction, coupled with its new alliance with Avigdor Lieberman's Yisrael Beiteinu party, makes it even more unlikely.

It is conceivable that after examining the combined Likud-Beiteinu ticket, Israel's voters will hand the baton to the center-left, which generally accepts the principles of adjusted 1967 borders and a shared Jerusalem. But the odds are slim. The main opposition leaders seem unable to overcome their over-sized egos and present a united front. Besides, polls show the voters are in no mood for big concessions.

A Complicated Position

The biggest mystery in all this is what Netanyahu actually wants. He's on record accepting the principle of a Palestinian state alongside Israel. If he means it, the U.N. resolution should be welcome news. Practically speaking, it does nothing more than ratify the principle of statehood and set the table for negotiating the details. Moreover, it gives a boost to Palestinian Authority chief Mahmoud Abbas and his policy of peaceful coexistence, slowing the momentum of the rejectionist Hamas. Against all that, the technicality of bypassing the Oslo process is small stuff.

But Netanyahu's position is more complicated than that. Although he embraced the two-state idea in 2009, his government never endorsed it. His Likud party openly opposed it even before the November primary. He's never tried to win approval from the government or the party. Critics question whether he ever really meant it.

Then there's the matter of getting to the table. Netanyahu has called since taking office for negotiations without preconditions. Abbas has complained—most recently in a lengthy Yediot Aharonot interview in October—that Netanyahu's "no preconditions" actually meant dismissing all the progress made

Benjamin Netanyahu

Benjamin Netanyahu served as Israel's prime minister twice in two decades. A well-known hawk (someone who advocates using military force or warlike action in order to carry out foreign policy), Netanyahu contends that his main political goals over the years have been prosperity through freedom and peace through security. He has promoted new high-tech industries, a free market economy, and democracy as the means to a prosperous Israel, and he has been outspoken regarding Israel's foreign policy for decades. In a 2009 speech to the United Nations, he signaled his willingness to move forward in the ongoing peace processes between Israel and the Palestinians (an Arab people whose ancestors lived in the historical region of Palestine and who continue to lay claim to that land) by saying, "All of Israel wants peace.... And if the Palestinians truly want peace, I and my government, and the people of Israel, will make peace. But we want a genuine peace, a defensible peace, a permanent peace."

Netanyahu does not believe that Palestinians accept Israel as a state. He remains firm in his belief that certain conditions must be met by the Palestinians to ensure Israel's safety before Israel will agree to a self-governed Palestinian state in the West Bank and the Gaza Strip, Arab regions occupied by Israel after the 1967 Arab-Israeli War (known as the Six-Day War in Israel). His conditions have been unacceptable to the majority of Palestinians. The prime minister, who began his second term in 2009, has many supporters in Israel and the United States who view his hard-line approach as a necessity for Israel, but he has also drawn international criticism for standing in the way of the peace process.

Gale Cengage Learning,
Biography in Context Online, *2013.*

in 2008 talks between Abbas and former Israeli leader Ehud Olmert, and starting again from zero. Abbas cried foul and refused. President Barack Obama's settlement freeze idea was a clumsy attempt to sidestep that impasse.

Netanyahu's been saying ever since that Abbas refuses to negotiate. That's technically true. But Israel's military and intelligence leaders, both past and present, continuously urge Netanyahu to get back to the table, suggesting that they don't believe Abbas is the problem. Many of them privately say they think Netanyahu simply doesn't want a deal.

Negotiating a Deal

Abbas and Olmert both say they were about two months away from concluding a peace agreement when Olmert was forced from office by a scandal (he was later acquitted). Both sides had made extraordinary concessions. The result was a deal both could live with. The main outstanding issues were the fate of the Jewish West Bank city of Ariel and the precise number of refugees Israel would repatriate in a symbolic, one-time "right of return."

It's possible Netanyahu envisions a Palestinian state with far more limited borders than Olmert and Abbas discussed, with Israel keeping control of the Jordan Valley and extensive security zones in the West Bank, along with groundwater, airspace and the electronic spectrum. He may have thought he could stonewall until he lowered Palestinian expectations. He may have thought he could negotiate a deal and get his coalition partners to acquiesce without endorsing it, much like the emerging concordat between Abbas and the Khaled Meshal faction in Hamas.

If that was his hope, the events of late November have made his task much, much harder.

> "The United Nations General Assembly voted to grant the Palestinian Authority non-member observer state status, a step that will not bring us any closer to peace."

Palestinian Statehood Is Counterproductive and Blocks Peace Efforts

Hillary Clinton

Hillary Clinton is a former US senator, former First Lady, a presidential candidate, and former US secretary of state. In the following viewpoint, taken from a speech to supporters of Israel, she maintains that the United Nations General Assembly vote to grant the Palestinian National Authority (PA) nonmember observer state status will not bring the region any closer to peace. Instead, the Palestinians should be renewing efforts to negotiate directly with Israeli authorities to negotiate a lasting and just peace. Clinton contends that by pursuing unilateral action and abandoning direct negotiations, the Palestinians have complicated the peace process and created new challenges for the United Nations and for Israel. She reiterates US support for a two-state solution but urges the Palestinians to step back and carefully

Hillary Clinton, "Remarks at the Saban Center for Middle East Policy," US Department of State, November 30, 2012.

consider the path ahead. The US will work very hard to facili-
tate peace efforts, protect Israeli security, and secure a two-state
solution that benefits both Israel and the Palestinian people, she
maintains.

As you read, consider the following questions:

1. According to Clinton, how much has trade between the United States and Israel increased since 1985?

2. What percentage of the population of Gaza does the author say is under the age of eighteen?

3. In what Middle Eastern countries does the US support democratic transitions, according to Clinton?

We have a lot to celebrate, because for years we have told you, our Israeli friends, that America has Israel's back. And this month [November 2012], we proved it again. (Applause.) When Israel responded to a rain of rockets, when sirens sounded and schools emptied and air raid shelters filled, America's next move was never in question. President [Barack] Obama and I stood before the international community and supported Israel's right to defend itself from a threat no country would tolerate. The Iron Dome system—invented by Israel, underwritten by America—knocked rockets out of the sky like never before.

We supported regional and international efforts to de-escalate the conflict and then seized on a diplomatic opening when it came. Working closely with President Obama from halfway around the world, I left the East Asia Summit in Cambodia to fly to Tel Aviv, to drive to Jerusalem, to meet with the Prime Minister and members of the inner cabinet, to go the next day to Ramallah [in Gaza], then back to the Prime Minister's office, and then to Cairo, and we were able to play a role in enabling the ceasefire to occur. That fragile ceasefire is holding. The skies above Israel are clear. And we are beginning to see the efforts to rebuild and resume daily life. But the world knows—and always will know—that whenever Israel is threatened, the United States will be there.

The US-Israel Bond

Now, that's a good thing, because we believe in our shared values. We understand we both live in a complicated and dangerous world. We're in the midst of a transformative moment in the Middle East, one that offers as many questions—in fact more questions than answers—and one that poses new challenges to Israel's place in the emerging regional order. As the story unfolds, all of us must work together to seize the promise and meet these challenges of this dynamic, changing Middle East.

In the past month alone, we've seen both the promise and those challenges. We've seen post-revolutionary Egypt work with the United States to help Israel broker a ceasefire and protect Egypt's peace treaty with Israel. We have seen cutting-edge defenses protect Israel, cities and rural areas. We have seen Israel fight for and win a stop to rocket fire from Gaza. But we've also seen the challenge of turning a ceasefire into a lasting calm; of helping Palestinians committed to peace find a more constructive path to pursue it; of putting Israel's peace with Egypt on a stronger foundation; of making sure that Iran can never acquire a nuclear weapon. And just yesterday, as you know, the United Nations General Assembly voted to grant the Palestinian Authority non-member observer state status, a step that will not bring us any closer to peace.

When it comes to a region full of uncertainty, upheaval, revolution, this much is constant and clear: America and Israel are in it together. This is a friendship that comes naturally to us. Americans honor Israel as a homeland dreamed of for generations and finally achieved by pioneering men and women in my lifetime. We share bedrock beliefs in freedom, equality, democracy, and the right to live without fear. What threatens Israel threatens America, and what strengthens Israel strengthens us. Our two governments maintain not just the formal US-Israel Strategic Dialogue, but a daily dialogue, sometimes an hourly dialogue, at every level.

In a season of tight budgets, US assistance to Israel is at a record high. And over the past few weeks, I have heard from Israelis the gratitude they felt when, after hearing the sirens, they saw a second rocket launch, and knew that was the Iron Dome, making them safer. America has helped keep Israel's Qualitative Military Edge as strong as ever. And Prime Minister [Benjamin] Netanyahu has described our security cooperation and overall partnership with Israel as "unprecedented."

Our shared obsession with innovation is also bringing us closer together. Google Executive Chairman Eric Schmidt recently called Israel "the most important high tech center in the world, after the United States." So it is no surprise that our diplomatic challenge is not only about a dialogue of strategic and political interests, including not just our soldiers and our politicians, but increasingly including our techies and our venture capitalists and our entrepreneurs. And it's no surprise that since Israel signed America's first-ever Free Trade Agreement back in 1985, trade between us has increased from 5 billion to more than 35 billion.

But all that we hope to accomplish together depends on keeping Israelis safe to pursue their passions in peace and security. It depends on ensuring Israel's future as a secure, democratic, Jewish state. So tonight I want to speak about four of the goals that our countries must pursue together to make that happen in a new Middle East.

The First Shared Goal

First, Iranian-made missiles and rockets launched from Gaza at Tel Aviv and Jerusalem only drove home what we already know: America, Israel, and the entire international community must prevent Iran from acquiring a nuclear weapon. (Applause.) This is a commitment that President Obama has made and repeated, because we know very well the Iranian regime already exports terrorism, not only to Israel's doorstep, but across the world. If we had a map I could put up there, I could show you what we track and plot on that map—the evidence of terrorism—mostly, thankfully, plots foiled or unsuccessful. Unfortunately, as in Bulgaria, some that succeeded. But those plots, those activities of Iran directly and through their agents, stretches from Mexico to Thailand.

We see Iran bringing repression to Syria. We see Iran brutalizing their own people. So a nuclear Iran is not simply a threat to Israel. It is a threat to all nations and risks opening the floodgates on nuclear proliferation around the world. When it comes to Iran's nuclear threat, the United States does not have a policy of containment. We have a policy of prevention, built on the dual tracks of pressure and engagement, while keeping all options on the table.

The United States is ratcheting up the pressure to sharpen the choices facing Iran's leadership. We've had our own sanctions in place for many years. But we never had a coalition like the one we have built over the last four years. We convinced all 27 nations of the European Union to stop importing Iranian oil and all 20 major global importers of Iranian oil—including Japan, India, China, and Turkey—to make significant cuts. Iran today exports more than one million fewer barrels of crude each day than it did just last year [in 2011]. Iran's currency is worth less than half of what it was last November. The pressure is real and it is growing.

And let me add, we take pride in the coalition we have assembled, but no pleasure in the hardship that Iran's choices have caused its own people to endure. We are making every effort to ensure that sanctions don't deprive Iranians of food, medicines, and other humanitarian goods. I travel the world working to help people everywhere take part in the global economy, and we never lose sight of the fact that Iranians deserve this no less than any other people.

America's goal is to change the Iranian leadership's calculus. We have worked with the P-5+1 [the five permanent members of the UN Security Council plus Germany] to put a credible offer on the table. If there is a viable diplomatic deal to be had, we will pursue it. And should Iran finally be ready to engage in serious negotiations, we are ready. When Iran is prepared to take confidence-building measures that are verifiable, we are prepared to reciprocate. What we will not do is talk indefinitely. The window for negotiation will not stay open forever. President Obama has made that clear, and by now I think it should be clear this is a President who does not bluff. He says what he means, and he means what he says.

The Second Shared Goal

The second shared goal I want to discuss is this: Now that rocket fire from Gaza has stopped, America and Israel have to work together with partners in the region to turn the ceasefire into a lasting calm. Now, we have no illusions about those who launched the rockets. They had every intention of hiding behind civilians in Gaza and killing civilians in Israel. And they would have killed more of each if they could have. They even fired poorly aimed rockets at Jerusalem, endangering Palestinians as well as Israelis, Muslim holy sites as well as those of Christians and Jews. As we said throughout the crisis, Israel retains every right to defend itself against such attacks.

But a lasting ceasefire is essential for the people of Israel, whose communities lie in the path of these rockets. The people of Gaza deserve better, too. Half the Gaza population are under the age of 18. These children, who didn't choose where they were born, have now seen two military conflicts in the last four years. Like all children, our children, they deserve better. Just as Israel cannot accept the threat of rockets, none of us can be satisfied with a situation that condemns people on both sides to conflict every few years.

Those who fire the rockets are responsible for the violence that follows, but everyone, all parties in the region, and people of good faith outside of the region, have a role to play in keeping or making peace. Israel can keep working energetically with Egypt to implement the ceasefire to keep the rockets out but also work to try to advance the needs of the people of Gaza. For its part, Egypt can use its unique relationship with [Palestinian militant Islamist party] Hamas and the other Palestinian factions in Gaza to make clear that it opposes provocation and escalation on its borders. And we look to Egypt to intensify its efforts to crackdown on weapon smuggling from Libya and Sudan into Gaza. I am convinced that if more rockets are allowed to enter Gaza through the tunnels, that will certainly pave the way for more fighting again soon. We are ready to help and to support Egyptian efforts to bring security and economic development to the Sinai.

Others who are close to Hamas and the other factions in Gaza, including Turkey and Qatar, can and should make clear that another violent confrontation is in no one's interest. Hamas itself, which has condemned those it rules to violence and misery, faces a choice between the future of Gaza and its fight with Israel. America has shown that we are willing to work with Islamists who reject violence and work toward real democracy. But we will not, we will never, work with terrorists. Hamas knows what it needs to do if it wishes to reunite the Palestinians and rejoin the international community. It must reject violence, honor past agreements with Israel, and recognize Israel's right to exist.

The Third Shared Goal

Of course, the most lasting solution to the stalemate in Gaza would be a comprehensive peace between Israel and all Palestinians, led by their legitimate representative, the Palestinian Authority. Which brings me to the third goal we must pursue together: At a time when violence commands attention,

How the Unites Nations Voted on Palestinian Statehood

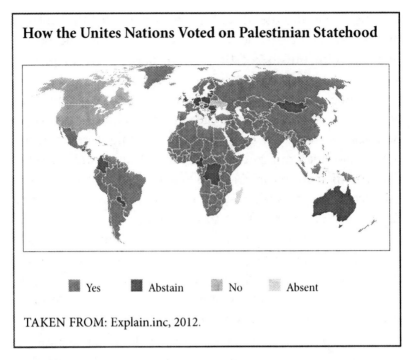

☐ Yes　　☐ Abstain　　☐ No　　☐ Absent

TAKEN FROM: Explain.inc, 2012.

America and Israel must do better at demonstrating not just the costs of extremism but the benefits of cooperation and co-existence.

For example, we have to convince Palestinians that direct negotiations with Israel represent not just the best but the only path to the independent state they deserve. America supports the goal of a Palestinian state, living side by side in peace and security with Israel. But this week's vote at the UN won't bring Palestinians any closer to that goal. It may bring new challenges to the United Nations system and for Israel.

But this week's vote should give all of us pause. All sides need to consider carefully the path ahead. Palestinian leaders need to ask themselves what unilateral action can really accomplish for their people. President [Mahmoud] Abbas took a step in the wrong direction this week. We opposed his resolution. But we also need to see that the Palestinian Authority in the West Bank still offers the most compelling alternative to rockets and permanent resistance.

At a time when religious extremists claim to offer rewards in the hereafter, Israel needs to help those committed to peace deliver for their people in the here and now. The leaders of the West Bank—President Abbas and Prime Minister [Salam] Fayyad—deserve credit for their real achievements on the ground. They made their streets safe again; they brought a measure of peace; they overhauled governing institutions. They have cooperated with Israel to help enhance Israel's security. And we have to be honest with ourselves that, right now, all of this needs our political and economic support to be sustainable. It also needs a political horizon.

So particularly in light of today's announcement [of the PA being granted nonmember observer state status], let me reiterate that this Administration—like previous administrations—has been very clear with Israel that these activities set back the cause of a negotiated peace. We all need to work together to find a path forward in negotiations that can finally deliver on a two-state solution. That must remain our goal. And if and when the parties are ready to enter into direct negotiations to solve the conflict, President Obama will be a full partner.

Now, some will say that, given the disappointments of the past and the uncertainties of today, now is not the time even to contemplate a return to serious negotiations, that it should be enough for Israel just to muddle through dealing with whatever crisis arises. But the dynamics of ideology and religion, of technology and demography, conspire to make that impossible. Without progress toward peace, extremists will grow stronger, and moderates will be weakened and pushed away.

Without peace, Israel will be forced to build ever more powerful defenses against ever more dangerous rockets. And without peace, the inexorable math of demographics will, one day, force Israelis to choose between preserving their democracy and remaining a Jewish homeland. A strong Israeli military is always essential, but no defense is perfect. And over the long run, nothing would do more to secure Israel's future as a Jewish, democratic state than a comprehensive peace.

The Fourth Shared Goal

And that leads me to my fourth goal. At a time when the Arab world is remaking itself right before our eyes, America and Israel have to work together to do what we can to ensure that democratic change brings the region closer to peace and security, not farther away. But there is no going back to the way things were. We are not naive about the risks these changes are bringing. And we recognize that for Israel, they hit close to home.

And so, even as the United States supports democratic transitions in Egypt and Tunisia, in Libya and Yemen, we are also making clear that rights and freedoms come with responsibilities. All states must address threats arising from inside their borders; fight terrorism and extremism; and honor their international commitments. And working closely with them on these critical issues does not mean we seek a return to the old bargain. Honoring obligations abroad does not lessen the need for these governments to respect fundamental rights, build strong checks and balances, and seek inclusive dialogue at home.

Egypt's recent declarations and the decision to hold a vote on the constitution, despite social unrest and a lack of consensus across Egypt's political spectrum, raise concerns for the United States, the international community, and most importantly for Egyptians. To redeem the promise of their revolution, Egypt will need a constitution that protects the rights of all, creates strong institutions, and reflects an inclusive process. Egypt will be strongest—and so will our partnership—if Egypt is democratic and united behind a common understanding of what democracy means. Democracy is not one election one time. Democracy is respecting minority rights;

democracy is a free and independent media; democracy is an independent judiciary. Democracy requires hard work, and it only begins, not ends, with elections. And let me add that the work of building consensus does not belong to new democracies alone. America will need broad-based support to end our impasse over our budget. Israel will need the same to solve your challenges.

Next door, the Syrian people are fighting for their rights and freedoms. A violent struggle against a tyrant is unfolding so close to Israel you can see it from the hilltops of the Golan Heights. Instability in Syria threatens all of us. But the safest and best path forward for Syria and its neighbors is to help the opposition build on its current momentum and bring about a political transition within Syria. The United States is using humanitarian aid, non-lethal assistance to the opposition, intensive diplomatic engagement, working with the Syrian people to try to bring about that political transition.

A Challenging Time

So there's a lot on our plates. And for me, this is a remarkable moment in history, if we were just to step back for a time and look at what is happening around the world. But it is also a time that is fraught with anxiety and insecurity, uncertainty, and danger. So we need to strengthen our consultations and collaboration on all of the issues that we face together. And we need to support the men and women in our militaries, in our diplomacy, who represent the United States and Israel at every turn so well. There is a lot of hard work ahead of us. But for me, there is no doubt that, working together, we are up to whatever task confronts us.

Protecting Israel's future is not simply a question of policy for me, it's personal. I've talked with some of you I've known for a while about the first trip Bill [Clinton] and I took to Israel so many years ago, shortly after our daughter was born. And I have seen the great accomplishments, the pride of the desert blooming and the start-ups springing up. I've held hands with the victims of terrorism in their hospital rooms, visited a bombed-out pizzeria in Jerusalem, walked along the fence near Gilo. And I know with all my heart how important it is that our relationship go from strength to strength.

As I prepare to trade in my post as Secretary of State for a little more rest and relaxation, I look forward to returning to Israel as a private citizen on a commercial plane—(laughter)—walking the streets of the Old City, sitting in a cafe in Tel Aviv, visiting the many Israelis and Palestinians I've gotten to know over the years. And of course, it is no state secret that I hope to become a grandmother someday. (Laughter.) And one day, I hope to take my grandchildren—(laughter)—to visit Israel, to see this country that I care so much about. And when I do, I hope we will find a thriving Israel, secure and finally at peace alongside a Palestinian state, in a region where more people than ever before, men and women, have the opportunity to live up to their God-given potential. That, and nothing less, is the future we must never stop working to deliver.

"If Palestinians had their own state . . . it would enable Palestinians to negotiate from a more equal position."

Palestinian Statehood Is Just and Affirms the Legitimacy of Palestine

Pierre Tristam

Pierre Tristam is a journalist and the editor of FlagerLive.com, a nonprofit online news source. In the following viewpoint, he supports the Palestinian attempt to gain recognition as a state at the United Nations, arguing that it is a necessary step for Palestinian self-determination and independence. Statehood would also enable the Palestinians to negotiate with Israel from a stronger and more equitable position. Tristam derides US opposition to the UN resolution, finding it hypocritical in light of US support for other fledgling Middle Eastern democracies and US democratic ideals. He predicts that US opposition will result in declining American credibility in the region.

As you read, consider the following questions:

1. According to Tristam, how long did it take Harry Truman to recognize Israel's existence?

2. When does Tristam say that both the Palestinian Authority and the Palestinian Liberation Organization formally recognized Israel's right to exist?

3. Why does President Obama oppose Palestinian independence in part, according to the author?

On May 14, 1948, the leaders of Jewish statehood in Palestine gathered at the Tel Aviv Museum to hear David Ben Gurion read a declaration of independence. After 32 minutes, Ben-Gurion said: "The State of Israel has arisen. The meeting is over." That was it. Israel was born. It took the say so of a few men convinced that their nation's time for self-determination had come. They didn't need the United Nations' partition [of Palestine] map. They didn't need Arab recognition. They certainly weren't going to let Arab hostility stop them. It took [US president] Harry Truman just 11 minutes to recognize Israel's existence.

A Shameful Move

It has taken Israel and the United States 63 years, and counting, to recognize Palestinians' equal right to exist. The Obama administration, shamelessly and unpardonably, is about to make matters worse by blocking a Palestinian attempt to gain recognition as a state at the United Nations. The administration's pandering to Israel and its contempt for the principles of our own Declaration of Independence will demolish what's left of its credibility in an Arab world daily being remade along principles America is abandoning.

In the United States and Israel, the story goes that it's Palestinians who deny Israel's right to exist. A minority of Palestinians do, and only on paper and in their blinkered, bigoted fantasies. A majority of them have long ago recognized that opposing Israel's right to exist is like imagining that the sky can be turned green. It won't happen. The Palestinian Authority and the PLO [Palestine Liberation Organization] formally recognized Israel's right to exist in 1993 and renounced terrorism. Hamas, the break-away militant organization, continues to reject Israeli existence, but with about as much hope of carrying through that rejection as nutty Texans have of one day being their own state again. It's an idiot's fantasy.

Israel, on the other hand, has brutally denied *Palestinians'* right to exist—not just in words, but in every reality that counts, by denying them a country of their own, a history, a culture, an identity (it's an Israeli fancy that Palestine and Palestinians as such have never and do not exist), by continuing to oppress, humiliate and kill them, as illegitimate military occupations usually do. Their homes are demolished, their properties expropriated, their lands diminished by the continued illegal colonization of East Jerusalem and the West Bank by Israeli occupiers still euphemistically but inaccurately referred to as "settlers." The euphemism is accepted practice in every American media, a complicity to injustice—and an overt bias—that goes unremarked, as do other distortions.

A Distorted View

Palestinians, overwhelmingly civilians, have been killed at six times the rate of Israelis since 2000, and double the rate since the end of Israel's last bloodletting—the barbaric assault on Gaza at the end of 2008 and the beginning of 2009. Specifically, Israeli forces have killed 227 Palestinians since that assault, most of them civilians. Israeli civilians have murdered six additional Palestinians. In comparison, Palestinians have killed 16 Israeli civilians and four Israeli soldiers, for a total of 20 Israelis, a ratio of almost 12-to-1. The numbers alone are terrorizing, to say nothing of the human cost. But the American press still manages to portray the situation as a lopsided pity for a besieged Israel, its back against an imaginary wall.

One wall is there, of course. Israel built it around Palestinian portions of the West Bank, a wall no less sordid than the Soviet one that once divided Berlin. Israel hasn't needed to build a wall around Gaza. It maintains a blockade there by sea, air, tanks and infantry, creating, in the words of the Turkish prime minister, "an open-air prison." You can't blame Palestinians for saying: enough.

In a few days, Palestinians at the United Nations are going to call for a vote on statehood. They're turning the tables on 1948. Almost every nation on earth will be supportive except two: Israel and the United States. The Obama administration is putting on a strange spectacle as it tries desperately to avert that vote and convince the Palestinians not to do what every fiber of American principle ought to be supporting and celebrating for the Palestinians: a declaration of self-determination and independence. Obama's posse is arguing against evidence that the only just course is face-to-face negotiations, as if that would be nullified if Palestinians had their own state. Of course it wouldn't be: it would enable Palestinians to negotiate from a more equal position, an equality Israel dreads and has been denying them, with American help, all along. Besides, Obama came to power raising expectations that he *would* get Palestinians and Israelis to the negotiating table, ending eight wasted years under George W. Bush, whose lip service to the Palestinian-Israeli conflict was Obamesque.

Hypocritical strategy

The Obama administration is pulling its latest denial of Palestinian rights even as it's been backhandedly supporting the aspirations of the Arab spring and the overthrow of tyrannies in Tunisia, Egypt, Libya and Yemen, though you can't accuse Obama of being consistent on the matter. He talks a good game of condemning the Syrian regime's murders of its own people, but sends an envoy to kiss the ring of the Bahraini king who has been doing the same thing with his people. He looks the other way when Bahrain calls on Saudi tanks to help with the skull-crushing (understanding that most of Saudi Arabia's military is American-built and American-trained).

The difference is that the United States depends on Bahrain to host the Navy's 5th Fleet in the Persian Gulf. And Obama continues to give Saudi Arabia, the Middle East's most repressive and backward nation—socially, politically, religiously—a pass.

Obama came to office portraying himself as Palestinians' best hope for independence. He's turned into just another obstructionist. He opposes Palestinian independence in part because he worries about losing the Jewish vote in Florida in 2012. How low his sights have fallen, though on that score he has the majority of the American public with him: the untenable contradiction between brandishing American ideals for everyone else while denying them for Palestinians is one Israeli import that remains recession- and reality-proof. The outcome will be ruinous, but self-inflicted.

Periodical and Internet Sources Bibliography

The following articles have been selected to supplement the diverse views presented in this chapter.

Yossi Beilin	"Support Palestinian Statehood," *New York Times*, November 25, 2012.
Alan Dershowitz	"The United Nations Should Not Recognize an Apartheid, Judenrein, Islamic Palestine," Gatestone Institute, September 21, 2011. www.gatestoneinstitute.org.
The Economist	"Yes to Palestinian Statehood," September 24, 2011.
Morton A. Klein	"Palestinian State Won't Bring Peace," Jewish News Service, July 14, 2013. www.jns.org.
Daoud Kuttab	"The Case for Palestine," Project Syndicate, November 27, 2012. www.project-syndicate.org.
Chris McGreal	"UN Vote on Palestinian Statehood Just Another Cautious Step Forward," *The Guardian* (Manchester, UK), November 29, 2012.
Rick Richman	"'Palestine' Does Not Qualify as a 'State,'" *Commentary*, November 13, 2012.
Brett D. Schaefer and James Phillips	"'No' to Palestinian Statehood," Heritage Foundation, November 29, 2012. www.heritage.org.
Sandy Tolan	"It's the Occupation, Stupid," TomDispatch.com, September 22, 2011.
John V. Whitbeck	"The West Should Accept Palestine's Right to Exist," *Huffington Post*, November 29, 2011. www.huffingtonpost.com.
Ali Younes	"Palestinian Statehood Is a Matter of Justice," *Palestine Chronicle*, September 21, 2011.

OPPOSING
VIEWPOINTS®
SERIES

CHAPTER 3

How Can Circumstances in the Palestinian Territories Be Improved?

Chapter Preface

On May 4, 2011, a ceremony was held in Cairo, Egypt, to sign a reconciliation agreement signaling the end to the divisive fight between Hamas and Fatah, the two main political factions in the Palestinian Territories. The four-year conflict had been so disruptive and damaging to the prospect of Middle East peace that some had begun to refer to it as the Palestinian Civil War. For many observers, the conflict between Fatah and Hamas was too complicated and deep-seated to be resolved easily. The announcement of a reconciliation was good news to many, especially for Arabs in the region; for others, however, it raised concerns about the future of Israeli-Palestinian relations.

At the ceremony, Palestinian Authority president Mahmoud Abbas asserted in his opening address that the rival factions were turning a page in the conflict in order present a unified front against the bigger issue: the creation of a Palestinian state and the end of Israeli occupation. "Four black years have affected the interests of Palestinians," he lamented. "Now we meet to assert a unified will. . . . Israel is using the Palestinian reconciliation as an excuse to evade a peace deal. Israel must choose between peace and settlement."

In the few years after the signing of the Cairo Agreement, the relationship between Fatah and Hamas encountered some turbulence. By 2012, it was apparent that the Cairo Agreement had stalled, and Hamas and Fatah signed another reconciliation agreement in Doha, Qatar, in 2012. According to reports, efforts to unify the two factions have largely failed, reviving tensions in the region and leading to further political and economic instability in the West Bank and the Gaza Strip.

The Fatah-Hamas conflict exploded in 2006, when Hamas won more seats than Fatah did in the legislative election and earned the right to form a new government. The United States,

Israel, and a number of other countries around the world expressed concern at the Hamas victory. Founded in 1987, Hamas is a Sunni Islamist group that has rejected Israel's right to exist and is regarded by many in the West as a terrorist organization. It is often associated with the Muslim Brotherhood, another Sunni Islamist group based in Egypt. For Israel and many others, handing Hamas the reins of power in Gaza and the West Bank would be very dangerous to Israeli national security.

Early on in its history, Fatah was also considered to be a violent enemy of Israel and a terrorist group. Established in 1965, Fatah eventually moderated its views and became the dominant political party in Palestinian politics under the leadership of its popular leader, Yasser Arafat. After his death in 2004, Fatah was weakened by internal dissension. By the 2006 elections, Hamas was on the rise and ready to challenge Fatah for leadership of the Palestinian people.

The Hamas victory led to a political crisis. Fatah and Hamas forces fought in the streets, leading to a decisive split: Hamas wrestled control of the Gaza Strip from Fatah and set up a government to rule the region whereas Fatah retained control of the West Bank. Yet repeated clashes and guerrilla attacks by groups associated with organizations have resulted in constant tension between the two factions.

The 2011 Cairo Agreement was in part an attempt to deal with that tension and unify the two warring parties. The Fatah-Hamas reconciliation is one of the subjects of the following chapter, which debates ways to improve the situation in the Palestinian Territories. Other viewpoints in the chapter examine the possibility of dissolving the Palestinian Authority, pressuring it to recognize Israel as a Jewish state, and the efficacy of building new institutions and strengthening existing ones to improve Palestinians' circumstances.

| "The logic of dissolving the Palestinian Authority is so clear that one wonders why [its leader] has not taken this step."

The Palestinian Authority Should Be Dissolved

Steven A. Cook

Steven A. Cook is an author and senior fellow for Middle Eastern Studies at the Council on Foreign Relations. In the following viewpoint, he states that the most effective way for the Palestinian leadership to force Israel to the negotiating table to obtain their independence is to dissolve the Palestinian Authority (PA). Cook outlines the advantage of such an extreme move: first, it might create a more favorable political environment for negotiation, and second, it will end the promise of the Oslo Accords and the idea of Palestinian sovereignty in the West Bank. The sooner that Israel is put on notice that it will be responsible for administering the West Bank, the sooner it will come back to the negotiating table. A drastic move is needed to break the current impasse and renew any prospects for a just and meaningful peace, Cook maintains.

As you read, consider the following questions:

1. According to Cook, what happened after the death of a young Palestinian activist, Arafat Jaradat, in February 2013?

2. What three figures does the author credit for thinking up the Oslo Accords?

3. What happened to the Palestinian Authority after the death of Yasser Arafat, according to Cook?

Negotiation? Done it. Violence? Check. Spoken openly of a one-state solution? Already part of the playbook. Declared statehood? A few times. UN recognition? In the bag. In the last almost decade and a half, the Palestinians have tried almost everything to force the Israelis to be more forthcoming on the issues that divide them—settlements, refugees, Jerusalem—all to no avail. For a combination of political reasons and security concerns the Israeli leaders have resisted the pressure, arguing either that the Palestinians cannot deliver or that Israel will not respond to threats. Indeed, the Israelis have been ruthlessly effective in demonstrating to the Palestinians that these tactics do not work through violence, settlements, and economic pressure. The result has been a crippled Palestinian leadership and bred despair among both West Bankers and Gazans.

Limited Options

What then should the Palestinians do? There are dire warnings that a third intifada—which observers have been predicting for years—is imminent. The death of a young Palestinian activist, Arafat Jaradat, at Israel's Megiddo prison [in late February 2013] led to clashes between Palestinians and Israeli security forces and settler violence heightened these concerns, but the fact of the matter is that the situation in the West Bank has been deteriorating for months. Palestinian President

The Oslo Accords

The Oslo Accords of 1993, which were negotiated between Israel and the Palestine Liberation Organization, led to the creation of the Palestinian National Authority, a quasi-governmental body with limited powers in Gaza and a patchwork of disconnected areas in the West Bank. The Palestinian National Authority, as the possible nucleus of an eventual Palestinian government, has received international funding from states supporting a two-state solution; for example, in 2007–2008, according to U.S. President George W. Bush (1946–), the United States gave over $190 million to the organization, lifting a funding ban imposed in 2006 after the militant group Hamas won dominance over the Palestinian National Authority in elections.

Gale Cengage Learning,
Global Issues in Context Online Collection, *2013.*

Mahmoud Abbas should do what he can to put a lid on the tension, but not because the Israeli government has made "an unequivocal demand to calm the territory" along with the promise of $100 million in tax revenue that Israel collects on behalf of the Palestinians. Rather, there is a potentially more effective way for the Palestinian leadership to deal with their present circumstances: Abbas should declare the Palestinian Authority (PA) closed for business. The benefits of dissolving the PA are twofold. First, the Palestinians might actually create a more favorable political environment for negotiations. Second, if it does not force Israel's hand, the end of the Palestinian Authority will finally bring [the 1993] Oslo [Accords] (remember that?) and the fiction of Palestinian sovereignty in the West Bank to an end.

The Oslo Accords

There is little doubt that twenty years ago when Yair Hirschfeld, Ron Pundik, and Ahmed Qurei dreamed up the Oslo Accords, which was a negotiating process, they hoped the Palestinian Authority would be the basis for the state that was to emerge in parts of the West Bank and Gaza Strip by May 1999. Yet Oslo made Palestinian statehood conditional upon Israeli consent and while Yasser Arafat proved to be a wholly irresponsible and inappropriate partner for peace and Abbas is perennially weak, Israel has done much to thwart what the Palestinian Authority was meant to do. First and foremost for the Israelis, the PA was a way of outsourcing the security functions of the Israel Defense Forces (IDF) in the West Bank and Gaza Strip. By the time the first intifada wound down in the early 1990s, Israelis had grown weary of policing the occupied territories and Israel's leaders were worried that putting down the uprising had sapped the IDF's ability to perform its core functions, protecting the country from attack. To paraphrase the late Yitzhak Rabin, "the PA would be there so we wouldn't have to be." As a result, an elaborate scheme of security cooperation was built into the follow-on to the original Oslo Accords.

The arrangements worked well for a while, but as time went on and the immediate promise and optimism of Oslo faded, the Palestinians were increasingly unwilling to do the Israelis' bidding on security. The first crack came in September 1996, pitting Palestinian paramilitary police against IDF soldiers. Despite efforts to re-establish security cooperation, the damage was done and whatever trust that had once existed between Israeli and Palestinian security forces was badly frayed. When the second intifada erupted in late 2000, Israel demanded that the PA "do more" to establish security even as the IDF systematically undermined the Palestinians' ability to establish order. Of course, by that time Arafat had come to believe that he had more to gain from the violence than from upholding Oslo, which from the perspective of the vast majority of Palestinians had been an abject failure. To be sure, there was a semblance of Palestinian self-government, but in the seven years between the time the Israelis and Palestinians initialed Oslo and the second intifada, the number of Israeli settlers grew considerably, leading Palestinians to conclude that the endless and inconclusive negotiations had been nothing more than a ruse.

An Obvious Step

The Palestinian Authority has limped along since the end of the second intifada and Arafat's death in 2004. Its functions are limited, Abbas is an afterthought in the region, and the prospects for a Palestinian-Israeli breakthrough are dimmer than ever. Declaring an end to the PA will either jolt the Israelis out of their complacency or lay bare the actual situation in the West Bank in which Israel has tightened its grip on the land that was supposed to be Palestine. By proclaiming the end of the Palestinian Authority, the Palestinians would be saying to the Israelis, "If you want to occupy the West Bank, it is yours, but do not expect us to administer it for you." The logic of dissolving the Palestinian Authority is so clear that one wonders why Abbas has not taken this step. After all, the PA is now little more than a vehicle to employ hundreds of thousands of Palestinians who draw their salaries and livelihoods from it and the international donors on which it depends. The idea that they could once again be primarily responsible for the Palestinian population should be enough to scare the Israelis into negotiation.

In the end, however, Abbas and his deputies are not going to put the Palestinian Authority out of business and hand the keys of the Muqata'a [headquarters] over to IDF commanders. Despite its decrepit state, the PA serves several important functions for them. Whatever shreds of power, international prestige, and riches Palestinian leaders in the West Bank still enjoy, they flow from the Palestinian Authority. It is a classic case of politicians doing something in their parochial interest that leads to a suboptimal outcome for the people they represent. For the rest of us, it just means that the fiction of Palestinian sovereignty and the policy distortions that come with it will continue.

| "The [Palestinian Authority] is not moribund. It can still make a difference."

The Palestinian Authority Should Not Be Dissolved

Dawoud Abu Lebdeh

Dawoud Abu Lebdeh is a political activist and the project manager for the Center for Democracy and Non-violence in Jerusalem. In the following viewpoint, he maintains that although the Palestinian Authority (PA) has failed to achieve its central goal—the implementation of a two-state strategy and a strong, independent Palestinian state—it should not be dismantled. He asserts that the PA should rethink its current strategy on the Palestinian issue and should continue to pursue the creation of a Palestinian state, but it should also lead a nonviolent resistance to Israeli occupation, he contends, concluding that a nonviolent campaign of mass civil disobedience will put pressure on Israel to come to the negotiating table on the issue of the two-state solution.

As you read, consider the following questions:

1. According to the author, price hikes on what main consumer items spurred recent demonstrations in the West Bank?

2. What 1993 agreement between Israel and the Palestine Liberation Organization (PLO) laid out the terms for Palestinian self-government in the West Bank and Gaza, according to Abu Lebneh?

3. How many Palestinians does the author estimate live in the West Bank and Gaza?

Last month [September 2012], large protests swept through major cities in the West Bank. In some places the demonstrations escalated into destruction of public property and a display of anarchy, while in others they were calm and collected. Peaceful or otherwise, the various demonstrations shared a common grievance: the economic policies of Prime Minister Salam Fayyad, recently highlighted after price hikes on main consumer items such as fuel and flour.

These protests have called into question whether the Palestinian Authority (PA) is still able to lead the Palestinian people.

The Future of the PA

Clearly the PA has reached a point where in order to survive and be effective it must rethink the strategy it has used until now. It has been 19 years since the Oslo Accord, the 1993 agreement between Israel and the Palestinian Liberation Organization (PLO) which laid out the terms for Palestinian self-government in the West Bank and Gaza, was signed; still, we, as Palestinians, do not have our own independent state. Perhaps it is time the PA considers abandoning these agreements and replacing them with an official policy of non-violent action against the Israeli occupation of the West Bank and Gaza.

The recent protests in the West Bank are an opportunity for the PA to rebuild its crumbling credibility with the Palestinian people. This lack of credibility was on full display in Nablus and Hebron where protestors aggressively called for the resignation of President Mahmoud Abbas and Prime Minister Fayyad, and the dismantling of the PA completely, while in Ramallah non-violent marchers called for an overhaul of the Palestinian Authority's economic and political policies.

I took part in a peaceful demonstration organized by the Palestine Youth Parliament in Ramallah. Our political message was a complex one. Members of the Youth Parliament did not blame solely the PA for the current economic problems, but also the Israeli Occupation. Demonstrators called for the cancellation of the Olso Accords and particularly the Paris Protocol, which set the terms for the current economic relationship between Israel and the Palestinian Authority. Published as an annex to the Olso Accords, it gave Israel control of the Palestinians' external trade as well as tax collection.

Today, the Palestinians are still living under occupation and continue to rely on support from donor countries in the West and several Arab countries to pay monthly salaries. A decision by donor countries to lower or withhold donations could bring the Palestinian economy to a collapse. In essence, the PA has been reduced to a mechanism that pays salaries to its employees and manages basic services in the Palestinian cities under its control.

Not the Envisioned Grand Future

This was not the grand future we envisioned when we supported the establishment of the PA almost 20 years ago. This should not have been the result of years of efforts to build up the institutions of a state. The PA is now facing a crossroads. Either it admits that it has failed to deliver independence based on a two-state solution with Israel and is dismantled, or it changes its thinking and strategy.

In my opinion the PA is not moribund. It can still make a difference. It should continue to pursue the state-building project that it began in 2006, but at the same time lead a non-violent resistance to the Occupation as official policy.

Up until today the non-violent movement in Palestine has been sporadic by nature—sometimes a top-down campaign, sometimes a grassroots swell. It is time for the PA to take up the non-violent struggle as an official means of putting pressure on Israel to agree to a two-state solution based on the 1967 borders with East Jerusalem as its capital.

For example, the PA, with the help of the PLO, could organize mass civil disobedience actions against Israel's occupation. With a million employees, the PA would not find it hard to ensure mass participation in these actions.

Many young people, like me, feel that a non-violent struggle is the only remaining tool in the shed. There are 4 million Palestinians in the West Bank and Gaza, and 77 per cent of them are under the age of 35. We have the resources to sustain an effective non-violent protest movement to show the world that we are serious and worthy of an independent, democratic state of our own.

The Palestinian people should not be calling for the PA to be dismantled. The alternative is worse. Let the PA show that it has its ear to the street, and let it take the lead in a non-violent struggle for independence.

"The Israeli government is correct to insist that the Palestinian Authority publicly recognize Israel as the Jewish state."

The Palestinian Authority Should Recognize Israel as a Jewish State

Jeff Jacoby

Jeff Jacoby is a columnist for the Boston Globe. *In the following viewpoint, he asserts that although the world recognizes that Israel is obviously a Jewish state, several Arab nations find Jewish sovereignty intolerable and continue to deny Israel's right to exist. Jacoby argues that that is why it is essential that the Palestinian Authority (PA) publicly recognize Israel as a Jewish state if the two countries are going to peacefully coexist. Such a move would be a huge step forward in the region. Israel has been both a Jewish state and a vibrant democracy, and its neighbors should recognize and accept that.*

As you read, consider the following questions:

1. What day does the author cite as the day Israel came into existence?

Jeff Jacoby, "The Undeniable Jewish State," *Boston Globe*, October 17, 2010. Reproduced with permission.

2. What kind of oath did Israel's parliament require in October 2010, according to the author?

3. According to Jacoby, what right does Bulgaria's constitution grant its citizens?

I s Israel a Jewish state?

Is the pope Catholic?

Nothing about Israel could be more self-evident than its Jewishness. As Poland is the national state of the Polish people and Japan is the national state of the Japanese people, so Israel is the national state of the Jewish people. The UN's 1947 resolution on partitioning Palestine contains no fewer than 30 references to the "Jewish state" whose creation it was authorizing; 25 years earlier, the League of Nations had been similarly straightforward in mandating "the establishment in Palestine of a national home for the Jewish people." When Israel came into existence on May 15, 1948, its Jewish identity was the first detail reported. The *New York Times's* front-page story began: "The Jewish state, the world's newest sovereignty, to be known as the State of Israel, came into being in Palestine at midnight upon termination of the British mandate."

Today, half the planet's Jews live in that state, many of them refugees from anti-Semitic repression and violence elsewhere. In a world with more than 20 Arab states and 55 Muslim countries, the existence of a single small Jewish state should be unobjectionable. "Israel is a sovereign state, and the historic homeland of the Jewish people," President Barack Obama told the UN General Assembly last month [September 2010]. By now that should be a truism, no more controversial than calling Italy the sovereign homeland of the Italian people.

The Root of the Arab-Israeli Conflict

And yet to Israel's enemies, Jewish sovereignty is as intolerable today as it was in 1948, when five Arab armies invaded the

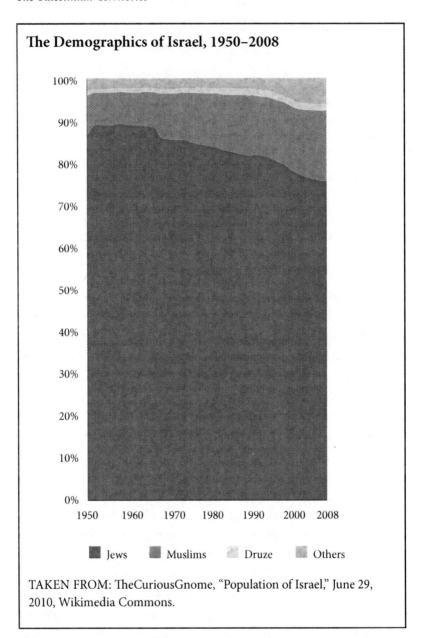

The Demographics of Israel, 1950–2008

Legend: Jews, Muslims, Druze, Others

TAKEN FROM: TheCuriousGnome, "Population of Israel," June 29, 2010, Wikimedia Commons.

newborn Jewish state, vowing "a war of extermination and a momentous massacre." Endless rounds of talks and countless invocations of the "peace process" have not changed the underlying reality of the Arab-Israeli conflict, which is not about settlements or borders or Jerusalem or the rights of Palestinians. The root of the hostility is the refusal to recognize the immutable right of the Jewish people to a sovereign state in its historic homeland. Until that changes, no lasting peace is possible.

That is why the Israeli government is correct to insist that the Palestinian Authority publicly recognize Israel as the Jewish state. It is *the* critical litmus test. "Palestinian nationalism was based on driving all Israelis out," [Arabic scholar] Edward Said told an interviewer in 1999, and the best evidence that most Palestinians are still intent on eliminating Israel is the vehemence with which even supposed "moderates" like [Palestinian leader] Mahmoud Abbas will not—or dare not—acknowledge Israel's Jewishness as a legitimate fact of life. "What is a 'Jewish state?'" Abbas ranted on Palestinian TV. "You can call yourselves whatever you want, but I will not accept it. . . . You can call yourselves the Zionist Republic, the Hebrew, the National, the Socialist [Republic]. Call it whatever you like. I don't care."

There are those who argue that Israel cannot be both a Jewish state and a democracy. When Israel's parliament decided last week [in mid-October 2010] to require new non-Jewish citizens to take an oath of allegiance to Israel as a "Jewish and democratic" state, some people bristled. "The phrase itself is an oxymoron," one reader wrote to the *Boston Globe*. "How can a state openly favor one ethnic group over all others and declare itself to be democratic?"

But there is no conflict at all between Israel's Jewish identity and its democratic values. Indeed, the UN's 1947 partition resolution not only called for subdividing Palestine into "independent Arab and Jewish states," it explicitly required each of them to "draft a democratic constitution" and to elect a government "by universal suffrage and by secret ballot." The Jews complied. The Arabs launched a war.

A Jewish State

Many of the world's democracies have official state religions. Think of Britain, whose monarch is the supreme governor of the Church of England: or of Greece, whose constitution singles out the Eastern Orthodox Church as the country's "prevailing religion." The linking of national character with religion is a commonplace. Israel stands out only because its religion is Judaism, not Christianity, Islam, or Hinduism.

Nor is democracy incompatible with ethnic or national distinctiveness. Ireland waives its usual citizenship requirements for applicants of Irish descent. Bulgaria's constitution grants the right to "acquire Bulgarian citizenship through a facilitated procedure" to any "person of Bulgarian origin." It is not oxymoronic to describe Ireland as "Irish and democratic" or Bulgaria as "Bulgarian and democratic." Israel's flourishing little Jewish democracy is no oxymoron either.

It is something different: a beacon of decency in a dangerous and hate-filled neighborhood. If the enemies of the Jewish state could only shed their malice, what an Eden that neighborhood could become.

> "[Hamas-Fatah] reconciliation is a pre-condition to any peace agreement and to stability in that region."

The Hamas-Fatah Reconciliation Is Crucial to the Middle East Peace Process

James Zogby

James Zogby is an author, political activist, and president of the Arab American Institute. In the following viewpoint, he is cautiously optimistic about a Hamas-Fatah accord, underscoring that the Palestinians need to be unified in order to move forward and achieve a Palestinian state. Zogby understands the concern over the role of Hamas, a political organization often viewed as terrorist, but stresses the need for all factions of the Palestinian polity to work together to achieve mutually-beneficial goals. He also hopes that by working with more mainstream political parties—like Fatah—Hamas will move to the middle and focus on making constructive progress in Palestinian independence. He notes that the prime minister of Israel, Benjamin Netanyahu, is hostile to the Fatah-Hamas reconciliation because he is opposed to a stronger, more unified effort for a Palestinian state and was hoping that the two factions would continue fighting amongst themselves instead of working together against Israel.

As you read, consider the following questions:

1. According to Zogby, what did Israeli prime minister Benjamin Netanyahu say about the possible Fatah-Hamas accord?

2. What two countries does the author identify as rejecting the results of the 2006 Palestinian election?

3. What does Zogby recommend that Arab states and others do to sustain the Palestinian Authority if the United States cuts aid?

The Israeli response to news that Palestinian factions had achieved a unity agreement was predictably irritating. Prime Minister Benjamin Netanyahu derided the agreement in stark terms, saying that the Palestinians had a choice of either "Peace with Israel or peace with Hamas". His spokesperson reduced this bumper sticker rejection of Palestinian unity even further to "reconciliation or peace".

What is, of course, galling is the assumption implicit in the prime minister's framing of the matter, namely, that peace with his government is a real possibility that the Palestinians have now rejected. In reality, the Netanyahu government has shown no interest in moving toward peace—unless on terms they dictate and the Palestinians accept.

While feigning disappointment at this Palestinian move, Netanyahu must privately be delighted. The pressure he was feeling to deliver some "concessions" to the Palestinians in his upcoming speech to the U.S. Congress has now been relieved. He can now revert to old form, expressing a vague desire for peace while warning that there is now clear evidence that there is no Palestinian partner with whom he can work.

For his part, Netanyahu will now feel free to accelerate tensions with Gaza, raids in the West Bank, home demolitions in Jerusalem and proceed with settlement construction, as he pleases. His allies in Congress will do the rest. They will denounce Palestinian reconciliation and claim that they have no choice but to take steps to suspend U.S. assistance to the Palestinian Authority.

Two Cautionary Notes

Nevertheless, what Fateh and Hamas have done in achieving their accord is important and should be supported. But two cautionary notes are in order: 1) They have merely announced an engagement—the wedding is scheduled down the road and the marriage will be fragile and subject to negative interference from obstructionists who will work hard to break it up; 2) the U.S. can be one of these home-wreckers (as we have been in the past) if the administration puts too much pressure on the Palestinians and/or supports Congress' efforts to deny them needed aid.

Because Palestine remains a captive nation, it is not the master of its fate. Prime Minister Salam Fayyed has done a brilliant job of reorganizing the P.A.'s [Palestinian Authority's] ministries and security forces and putting the Palestinians' financial house in order. But Gaza remains under a near total blockade; Jerusalem and its environs (once the Palestinian metropol—its religious, cultural, educational, economic and social hub) have been severed from the rest of the West Bank; and the West Bank, itself, has been separated into little cantons with no access or egress to the outside world. As a result no real or sustainable economy can develop, leaving Palestinians dependent on Israel and foreign aid. To punish a captive people by denying them aid would be cruel and most unhelpful.

Given this dire situation, to suggest that the Palestinians must choose reconciliation or peace, when peace has not been, and is not now, an option, is nothing more than a disingenuous and cruel taunt.

What has been so very clear since the elections of 2006 was that the Palestinian polity had been fractured and was in disarray—with everyone behaving badly. The U.S. and Israel did not accept the outcome of the election (that the [George W.] Bush administration had pushed for). Israel took repressive measures (at one point holding in detention, without charge, the majority of the newly elected Hamas legislature, making it impossible for that body to function). Aid was cut and the U.S. began to press the losing side, Fateh, to seek a confrontation. Hamas also behaved foolishly. Instead of assuming the role of a responsible government, and ignoring the many provocations against them, they continued their old violent behavior—resorting to terror and picking fights they couldn't win. The results were disastrous and for three years now the Palestinians were not only weak and occupied, but increasingly divided with two competing "governments" in two captive territories. This situation was both burdensome and unsustainable.

The Unity Factor

The Palestinians need this unity and, whether they know it or not, the U.S. and the Israelis need the Palestinians to be unified. Palestinian reconciliation is a precondition to any peace agreement and to stability in that region. Hamas (whose past behavior I deplore and whose politics I reject) is a real part of the Palestinian polity. The Bush administration's approach of working to deepen the internal Palestinian divide only aggravated the situation, creating more bitterness, and threatening to create a permanent rupture—a situation which would only benefit those who envision a long-term Israeli occupation and domination of a captive Palestinian people.

What Is Hamas?

Hamas is a militant Islamist organization that is opposed to the existence of Israel and its dominance over the Occupied Territories (also known as the Palestinian Territories). The organization functions as both a political and military entity. Hamas provides (or financially supports) such social services as education, medical care, food, and daycare to Palestinians and runs candidates for electoral offices in the Palestinian National Authority.

Hamas also wages war with Israeli armed forces and rival militant groups. It is also accused by many international governments and observers of committing or sponsoring acts of terrorism, most notably suicide bombings and firing rockets indiscriminately at southern Israel.

Palestinians are Arabs who live either in Israel's nearby states, including Jordan, or in the Occupied Territories—areas adjacent to Israel that Israel has controlled since 1967 . . . .

Most Palestinians in the Occupied Territories are poor, restricted in their movements, and angry at being expelled in 1948 from the area occupied by Israel. Although the Palestinian independence movement is dominated by political and strategic realists willing to compromise with Israel, Hamas and other militant groups such as the al-Aqsa Martyrs' Brigades recruit from among the most desperate and angry Palestinians. Hamas, the largest Palestinian militant group, has officially committed itself to Israel's destruction and calls for the establishment of an Islamic state covering all of Palestine.

Gale Cengage Learning,
Global Issues in Context Online Collection, *2013.*

This effort at reconciliation may now provide Palestinians an opportunity to get their house in order and to move Hamas in a more constructive direction. Those in Israel and in the Congress who are hyperventilating over Hamas' Charter [which pledges to destroy Israel] ought to read [Israeli ruling political party] LIKUD's and/or read some of the choice religious pronouncements coming from [Israeli ultraorthodox party] Shas' spiritual leader.

What should be of concern is Hamas' behavior, and this reconciliation agreement may yet prove to be the best way to guarantee that Hamas will act responsibly. If the new government of technocrats is allowed to function and to continue on the path laid out by Fayyed, and if Hamas and Fateh can continue to work out a modus operandi [method of operating] in their respective areas, leading to a new election later this year [2011], Palestinians will have put themselves in an even stronger position to claim statehood.

Bottom line: Palestinians shouldn't be asked to choose "reconciliation or peace" especially when the party doing the asking is denying them the chance to have both. Palestinians need both reconciliation and peace. They are working on the former. Now is the time for the U.S. and Israel to make a real contribution to advancing the latter.

In the short term, should the U.S. Congress suspend needed aid, it would be important for the Arab states and others to step up and sustain the P.A., allowing the reconciliation plan time to work through elections and an expected U.N. vote [on Palestinian statehood] in the fall. None of this, of course, will, by itself, result in a state. But a democratic and unified Palestinian Authority will make a stronger moral and legal case for recognition than Palestinians can make today living as they do divided and governed by entities of questionable legitimacy. Can this be why Israel is so hostile to the agreement?

> "Far from advancing peace, to encour-
> age Hamas-Fatah reconciliation . . .
> will accelerate conflict."

The Hamas-Fatah
Reconciliation: Threatening
Peace Prospects

Michael Rubin

Michael Rubin is an author, educator, and resident scholar at the American Enterprise Institute in Washington, DC. In the following viewpoint, taken from his testimony before a subcommittee of the US House of Representatives' Foreign Relations Committee, he views the accord between two Palestinian factions, Hamas and Fatah, to be a threat to peace prospects in the region. He predicts that Hamas's influence will radicalize Fatah and destabilize political order in the West Bank where Fatah dominates. Hamas, a determined foe of Israel, will not constructively engage in a meaningful peace process, contends Rubin. The Fatah-Hamas reconciliation could even destabilize other countries in the region, particularly Syria and Jordan, and negatively impact American interests in the region. Rubin urges the

Michael Rubin, "The Hamas-Fatah Reconciliation: Threatening Peace Prospects," American Enterprise Institute, February 5, 2013. Copyright © 2013 by the American Enterprise Institute. All rights reserved. Reproduced with permission.

United States to refrain from subsidizing any coalition govern-
ment made up of both Hamas and Fatah members, arguing that
it will only accelerate further conflict.

As you read, consider the following questions:

1. According to Rubin, when did the US Congress pass an anti-terrorism act formally declaring the Palestine Liberation Organization a terrorist group?

2. In what year does the author say that Congress passed the Middle East Peace Facilitation Act?

3. When did Hamas stage a violent putsch against Fatah to take control of Gaza, according to Rubin?

Chairwoman Ros-Lehtinen, Ranking Member Deutch, Honorable Members, thank you for the opportunity to testify before this Subcommittee today on this important topic.

Far from advancing peace, to encourage Hamas-Fatah reconciliation and to subsidize any coalition government will accelerate conflict. At issue is not only the sanctity of diplomatic agreements which form the basis for Middle East peace efforts, but also the outcome of a battle between more secular movements struggling against a radical Islamist revival.

The Obama Administration's desire to fund the Palestinian government does more harm than good not only to moderate Palestinians who desire to live in peace with Israel, but also to U.S. regional interests and prospects for Arab-Israeli peace.

At its core, American opposition to Hamas rests on two interconnected issues: First is Hamas' embrace of terrorism and second is the movement's refusal to honor diplomatic agreements signed by the Palestinian Authority.

The current debate about how to approach Fatah-Hamas reconciliation falls into a decades-long pattern of shifting goals posts and diluting demands in order to keep diplomacy alive. The record of the State Department's failure to hold its

Palestinian partners to their commitment to abandon terrorism is extensive, and its results clear: Absent a clear-cut, inalterable demand that the Palestinian groups first uphold their commitment to abandon terror, diplomacy will fail and the situation will worsen.

For decades, U.S. administrations considered the Palestine Liberation Organization (PLO) a terrorist group and rogue entity, unworthy of serious policy consideration. As former Secretary of State Henry Kissinger explained, "Before 1973, the PLO rarely intruded into international negotiations. In the 1972 communiqué ending Nixon's Moscow summit, there was no reference to Palestinians, much less to the PLO. . . . The idea of a Palestinian state run by the PLO was not a subject for serious discourse."[1] The reason for the PLO's lack of credibility among Western diplomats and policy makers was its refusal to abandon terrorism. While diplomats today insist it never hurts to talk, the damage from engaging an insincere partner can be huge. Throughout the PLO's early years, Chairman Yasser Arafat was explicit in his embrace of terrorism and his cynicism about the role of diplomacy. Addressing the United Nations, for example, he described diplomacy as a corollary to armed struggle. "We are also expressing our faith in political and diplomatic struggle as complements, as enhancements of armed struggle," he declared.[2]

The PLO's unapologetic embrace of terrorism did not dissuade some within the State Department from arguing for direct relations with the PLO, even before the group ostensibly abandoned terrorism as a result of the Oslo Agreement. During his 1980 presidential campaign, Ronald Reagan swore he would not negotiate with terrorists. The State Department had other ideas, though.[3] The fact that the PLO was a pariah, its influence had reached its nadir in the wake of its expulsion

1 Henry Kissinger, *Years of Upheaval.* (New York: Little Brown and Company, 1982), p. 625.
2 Speech by Yasser Arafat to the United Nations General Assembly, November 13, 1974.
3 Allan Gerson, *The Kirkpatrick Mission.* (New York: Free Press, 1991), p. 26, 42.

from Lebanon, and its execution of an elderly, wheelchair-bound American onboard the *Achille Lauro* had disgusted the international community, did not mean that diplomats were willing to give up hope to find a partner in the group. In 1985, for example, U.S. diplomats were willing to accept the fiction of a joint Jordanian-PLO delegation comprised almost exclusively of PLO members so long as Arafat accepted United Nations Security Council Resolution 242, renounced terror, and acknowledged Israel's right to exist. At the last minute, Arafat refused, and so talks were cancelled.[4] That willingness to cancel talks and, in the post-Oslo era, assistance is a thing of the past.

Because of the State Department's unwillingness to hold firm to declared principles if such a stand prevented more immediate dialogue, it is often Congress which intercedes to ensure that U.S. national security interests are upheld. In 1987, Congress passed an Anti-Terrorism Act which formally declared the PLO to be a terrorist organization for the purposes of U.S. law, and reinforced the prohibition on U.S. dialogue with the group, forcing the State Department to close the PLO's offices in Washington.

The PLO got a new lease on life in December 1987 with the outbreak of the first *Intifada*. While the uprising was a largely grassroots affair, senior diplomats believed it better to negotiate with the PLO's exiled leaders than with local Palestinian activists accustomed to working with Israelis. When proxies for the PLO met with National Security Council official Robert Oakley to seek talks, Oakley repeated U.S. preconditions: the Palestinians first must accept Resolutions 242 and 338, renounce terrorism, and accept Israel's right to exist.[5] While Fatah has, at various times, accepted such conditions rhetorically if not in reality, Hamas still refuses to do so.

4 Dennis Ross, *The Missing Peace*, (New York: Farrar, Straus, and Giroux, 2004), p.47.
5 Mohamed Rabie, *U.S.-PLO Dialogue*. (Gainesville: University Press of Florida, 1995), p. 14.

The sanctity of agreements underscores Western diplomacy, but too often the State Department ignores their violation in order to keep dialogue alive. Arafat and the PLO never placed the same premium on honesty: In the run-up to the Oslo Agreement and, arguably in its aftermath as well, the pattern was constant. Because Arafat remained directly complicit in terror, Congress in 1989 passed the PLO Commitments Compliance Act (PLOCCA) which required the State Department to affirm that the PLO was abiding by its commitment to abandon terrorism and recognize Israel's right to exist.[6] If the PLO did not meet its commitments, dialogue would cease. To keep dialogue alive, however, diplomats simply omitted reporting episodes which might lead to the cessation of dialogue.

The Oslo Accord changed U.S. engagement with the Palestinians forever. Rather than lead a terror group, Arafat would head a proto-government. In October 1993, Congress passed the Middle East Peace Facilitation Act, which waived prohibitions on contacts with the PLO, and allowed the organization to open its *de facto* embassy in Washington so long as the PLO continued to abide by its commitments to cease terrorism and recognize Israel.[7] Congress also enabled the president to waive legislation that prohibited U.S. government employees from negotiating with the PLO.[8]

As implementation of the Declaration of Principles floundered, the State Department's instinct was to seek quiet rather than enforce the agreement. When Arafat adopted a bizarre interpretation of his commitments, diplomats scrambled to appease him. After Arafat returned to Gaza, he reversed course on commitments to ensure security and revoke portions of the PLO's Charter which called for Israel's destruction. Because the State Department wanted to press forward with

6 Title VIII, P.L. 101–246, February 16, 1990.
7 The Middle East Peace Facilitation Act of 1993, P.L. 103–125, October 28, 1993.
8 Clyde Mark, "Palestinians and Middle East Peace: Issues for the United States," CRS Issue Brief for Congress, October 10, 2003. No. IB92052.

talks regardless of Arafat's backpedaling, Congress again acted. On July 15, 1994, the Senate prohibited release of taxpayer funds to the Palestinian Authority unless the PLO complied with its commitments to renounce and control terrorism.[9] Congressional action did not filter down to all diplomats in the region, though. "I took every opportunity I could to see Arafat," Edward Abington, Jr., the U.S. Consul General in Jerusalem, recounted, "I just felt it was important to be seen as very active, as understanding Palestinian positions, showing sympathy and empathy."[10]

The same debates regarding the place of commitments and accountability in the peace process continued into the Bush administration. After a wave of terrorist attacks followed Palestinian assurances that terror would cease, President George W. Bush had had enough. Engagement for engagement's sake had failed. He decided to take a zero tolerance approach. "There is simply no way to achieve peace until all parties fight terror," he declared, adding, "I call on the Palestinian people to elect new leaders, leaders not compromised by terror."[11] The State Department resisted Bush's new approach. "The Arabists in the State Department were appalled" by Bush's speech, then-National Security Advisor Condoleezza Rice recalled.[12] Amidst international criticism and resistance from within his own administration, though, Bush abandoned his principled stand, and the State Department quickly reverted to business as usual. A no-nonsense demand to end terrorism before diplomacy gave way to the Road Map, whose own benchmarks soon fell victim to a desire to keep the Palestinians at the table.

---

9 H.R. 4426, Foreign Operations, Export Financing, and Related Programs Appropriations Act, 1995, Public Law No: 103-306.

10 Jonathan Broder, "The American Diplomat in Arafat's Corner," *The Jerusalem Report*, April 10, 2000.

11 George Bush, "Rose Garden Speech on Israel-Palestine Two-State Solution," White House, June 24, 2002.

12 Condoleezza Rice, *No Higher Honor.* (New York: Crown Publishers, 2011), p. 145.

The Hamas-Fatah Accord

Hamas and Fatah reached an agreement on 27 April [2011] to end their four-year rift and form a unified Palestinian government. Under the terms of the agreement, reached in Egypt, a unity government will be formed and a date for new elections will be set. The Israeli government responded by saying that it would not negotiate with a government that included Hamas. U.S. officials also stressed that any Palestinian government must recognize Israel's right to exist and must renounce violence against Israel. On 5 May, a day after Fatah and Hamas signed a formal accord, a reporter asked Secretary of State Clinton if the accord meant the end of negotiations with Israel; Clinton said only that the U.S. government was "carefully assessing" the implications of the new reconciliation agreement.

"Hamas: Role and Influence,"
Global Issues in Context Online Collection, *2013*.

Enthusiasm for direct talks with Hamas increased after the group's victory in January 2006 elections. A number of journalists and analysts argued that political power might moderate Hamas,[13] and European officials urged Washington to forget Hamas' past.[14] Optimists ignored Hamas co-founder Mahmoud az-Zahar's promise: "We will join the Legislative Council with our weapons in our hands."[15] After more than seven years, there can no longer be any debate: Power has not moderated Hamas.

13 See, for example, Marina Ottaway, "Islamists and Democracy: Keep the Faith," *The New Republic*, June 6 and 13, 2005; and Claude Salhani, "Politics & Policies: U.S. Must Engage Hamas," United Press International, January 23, 2006.

14 Chris Patten, "Time to judge Palestine on its results," *Financial Times*, March 13, 2007.

15 Michael Herzog, "Can Hamas Be Tamed?" *Foreign Affairs*, March/April 2006.

When Hamas won a majority in the Palestinian Legislative Council, the United States and its Quartet partners, agreed diplomatic recognition of Hamas would be premature because of the group's refusal to recognize Israel, accept previous agreements, and forswear terror,[16] it was not long before first Turkey and then European foreign ministries began to shift their tune. When Hamas staged a violent putsch against Fatah in July 2007 to consolidate control over Gaza, European diplomats argued they had no choice but to engage Hamas since there was no longer any pretext of a Palestinian coalition.[17] Dialogue rather than peace had once again become diplomacy's goal.

Too often, be it with the PLO, Hamas, or Hezbollah, the passage of time rather than reform legitimizes dialogue in diplomats' eyes. It is a pattern which discourages reform and compromise: Engaging and legitimizing the most violent factions incentivizes terrorism and disadvantages groups which play by the rules. Diplomacy with terrorist groups can also throw a lifeline to movements which otherwise might peak and collapse.

It is impossible to consider today's reconciliation between Fatah and Hamas without reference to the broader context of the so-called Arab Spring. While the uprisings which sparked the Arab Spring had their roots in a desire among ordinary people for government accountability, it was not long before the Muslim Brotherhood and even more radical Islamist groups and Salafi movements hijacked the revolutions. These Islamist groups had two distinct advantages:

16 David Welch, assistant secretary of State for Near Eastern Affairs, Senate Committee on Foreign Relations, September 25, 2008.

17 Maurizio Caprara, "Non regaliamo Hamas ad Al Qaeda," *Corriere della Sera* (Milan), July 17, 2007; Mark Heller, "Should the European Union talk to Hamas?" *Transatlantic Issues*, No. 32, June 25, 2008; Carolin Goerzig, "Engaging Hamas: Rethinking the Quartet Principles," *ISS Opinion*, March 2010.

First, the Muslim Brotherhood had been in opposition for almost eight decades, during which time they could promise the world, without ever having to prove the efficacy of their ideas.

Second, Islamist movements did not have to operate on an even playing field: Not only rich Persian Gulf emirates like Qatar, but also nominal republics like Turkey lent considerable wealth to subsidizing the most radical Islamist groups. Turkish Prime Minister Recep Tayyip Erdoğan has made little secret of his ideological and religious affinity for both the Muslim Brotherhood and, in the context of Palestinian politics, Hamas as well.

Analysts often bifurcate the Middle East into competing groups: Sunnis versus Shi'ites, republics versus monarchies; dictatorships versus democracies; and Arabs versus non-Arabs. The overriding competition at present is between Islamists versus secular regimes. Iran may be largely Shi'ite and Egypt overwhelmingly Sunni, for example, but Tehran sees Cairo as a new ally in its fight against secularist regimes. Hamas' renewed empowerment comes not autonomously, but against the backdrop of Muhammad Morsi's rise in Egypt and Hamas' growing relations with Iran.

Fatah may not be moderate, but it is not Islamist and relative to Hamas it is restrained. Rather than see Hamas moderate in order to join a coalition with Fatah, the opposite will become true: Hamas will have doubled down on its rejectionism, while forcing Fatah to radicalize. To promote the two movements' reconciliation would effectively enable Hamas to subsume Fatah.

The results would be grave for the region: Should Hamas establish its dominance on the West Bank in addition to Gaza, not only would Israel face a growing threat, but Hamas and its allies would also move to destabilize the Kingdom of Jordan, perhaps America's chief Arab partner. Second- and third-order effects will severely undermine both prospects for peace and broader American interests in the region. Chaos in Syria and the radicalization of the Syrian opposition will only compound the problems.

Because money is fungible, it is impossible for the United States to support only Fatah elements should Fatah and Hamas govern together. U.S. foreign assistance should never be an entitlement, and it should never benefit groups which are endemically and inalterably hostile to the United States. The Oslo process established the Palestinian Authority on the basis of its recognition of Israel and the agreement to negotiate statehood and other issues at the diplomatic table. That conditionality infuses the Palestinian Authority's presence in the West Bank and Gaza. In theory, the Palestinian Authority has no right to exist should it obviate the Oslo Accord.

Diplomacy will fail when any figure, be it Mahmoud Abbas, Ismail Haniyeh, or Khalid Mishaal treats diplomatic commitments not as sacrosanct but as an *à la carte* menu from which to pick and choose. It will be hard to expect any government to place its security on the line for diplomatic assurances which in practice expire in less than two decades.

The Obama administration and American diplomats may believe they are charting a path to peace, but by turning a blind eye to accountability and treating U.S. assistance to Palestinian government as an entitlement, they are committing a grave strategic error which could permanently handicap prospects for peace and instead encourage a more devastating conflict.

"Relying on . . . Palestinian Prime Minister Salam Fayyad's program to build
a Palestinian state despite occupation
and internal division . . . will likely lead
to failure and disappointment."

Palestinian Attempts at Institution Building Do Not Solve the Region's Problems

Nathan J. Brown

*Nathan J. Brown is the author of several books on Arab politics
and is a professor of international affairs at the George Washington University in Washington, DC. In the following viewpoint,
he maintains that then Palestinian prime minister Salam
Fayyad's institution-building program does not offer an effective
solution to the deeper problems affecting Palestinian politics, including occupation, corruption, political division, and pervasive
institutional decay. For one, Fayyad's efforts are constrained by
economic, political, and social realities on the ground, particularly the authoritarian rule under which it operates. There is no*

Reprinted by permission of the publisher, from Nathan J. Brown, "Fayyad Is Not the
Problem, but Fayyadism Is Not the Solution to Palestine's Political Crisis" (Washington,
DC: Carnegie Endowment for International Peace, SEPTEMBER 17, 2010), http://
carnegieendowment.org/2010/09/17/fayyad-is-not-problem-but-fayyadism-is-not
-solution-to-palestine-s-political-crisis/1lu4#. Copyright © 2010 by Nathan J. Brown.
All rights reserved. Reproduced with permission.

quick fix to the Palestinian problem, but it is clear that building new institutions and improving existing ones is a limited solution and should be pursued along with other major structural reforms.

As you read, consider the following questions:

1. According to Brown, during what years did an elected Palestinian parliament draft a whole series of laws and empower a set of institutions?

2. How many areas was the West Bank divided into by the Oslo Accords, as stated by the author?

3. Why does Brown believe that democratic elections in Gaza will not happen under the current circumstances?

American policy makers have learned the hard way in Iraq and Afghanistan the costs of pretending that strong institutions and viable political processes are emerging; in both cases the institutions and processes actually being built sometimes had too loose a connection to politics on the ground. U.S. leaders have learned the mistakes of relying too heavily on attractive local interlocutors and treating them as surrogates for genuine institutional development and deeply-rooted political processes.

The Limitations of Fayyadism

But those lessons are being forgotten in Palestine. Relying on "Fayyadism"—Palestinian Prime Minister Salam Fayyad's program to build a Palestinian state despite occupation and internal division—alone will likely lead to failure and disappointment. Technocratic management can probably keep Palestinian institutions afloat and even improve their functioning in some limited ways. But it does not even pretend to offer a solution for the deeper problems afflicting Palestinian politics—division, repression, occupation, alienation, and wide-reaching institutional decay.

In short, Fayyadism might hold down the fort for a short period, but it will not deliver what its boosters promise. By pretending that Fayyadism, combined with Israeli-Palestinian diplomacy, is delivering a state, policy makers virtually ensure that the negative trends they are ignoring will confront them when they are least prepared for them. This is not to say that Fayyad should abandon his efforts or that international support for his cabinet and program should cease. But relying on Fayyadism alone to solve the challenges of Palestine will likely lead to failure and disappointment.

This was the conclusion of a paper I published two months ago [in July 2010]. The paper generated considerable attention and hit a sensitive nerve with supporters of Fayyadism. Understandably so. Critical political and financial support is at stake; questioning the program just as it generates sympathetic press coverage might be damaging indeed. But it is precisely because so much is at stake that we must be careful and realistic in understanding what Fayyadism can and cannot accomplish. Fayyad's efforts should continue to draw international help. But they should not be used as an excuse—as they are right now—for postponing and ignoring difficult political questions. The time to address the deep crisis in Palestinian politics is now.

I received a broad set of questions and criticisms about the paper, some of which reflect disquiet with the political implications of my analysis. It is easy to sympathize with those discomfited, and it therefore makes sense to respond to some of the questions and criticisms in the hopes of contributing to a more sound and accurate understanding of current political realities:

Impossible Circumstances

Isn't limited state building the best that can be accomplished under the impossible circumstances Fayyad faces? Should Fayyadism then be criticized for the circumstances under which it operates?

Fayyad does indeed operate under impossible conditions. Such an observation can generate empathy for him as an individual (and indeed, all the references to Fayyad's personal characteristics in my earlier paper were positive or neutral; his personality is an asset, not a problem). But viewing the issues through the lens of a single individual—and using his virtues as a surrogate for a viable policy—is precisely the problem with the current approach. It is based on either a shallow understanding or deep contempt for Palestinian politics.

In the three years since the West Bank–Gaza split, most trends for Palestinian politics and for peacemaking are negative—Hamas [ruling party of Gaza] is more deeply entrenched; Fatah [ruling party in the West Bank] is in deeper disarray; and Palestinian society strikes me as characterized far more by despair than by cheery responsiveness to Fayyad's programs.

Fayyad's accomplishments, like his virtues, are real—he has improved public administration, tiptoed into areas that are under direct Israeli security control, and marshaled impressive international diplomatic and financial support. The real political damage is done when those accomplishments are treated not as a way to keep Palestinian politics on life support but as a cure for the underlying diseases. Hamas, Gaza, authoritarianism, and political decay will not be easier issues to deal with if we project current trends a year or two into the future.

And in the meantime, the Palestinian cabinet is severely limited in what improvements it can provide. The latest set of promises in the program for the next year of "state building" coincidentally focuses on precisely those areas—legal reform and education—analyzed in my paper. I showed how only limited and technical improvements had been accomplished in those areas (with some areas of regression as well in both) and why it would be difficult to move beyond them.

Structural Problems

In general, Fayyadism runs into two deep structural problems. First, what it can accomplish is inherently limited by the authoritarian political context in which it operates. When Palestinian democracy, as problematic as it was, operated with an elected parliament from 1996 to 2006, deputies with a parliamentary mandate drafted a whole series of laws and empowered a set of institutions. Fayyadism may rescue parts of that project, but it cannot extend it very far. For instance, the Palestinian Legislative Council elected in 1996 drafted a comprehensive criminal code but did not complete the work. Now the two Palestinian governments—the one in Gaza and the one in Ramallah—have shown some interest in reviving the comprehensive code in order to cement their separate state-building efforts. But neither can do so in a legitimate way because neither has more than an ad hoc (and legally dubious) legislative process. Fayyad's cabinet has been able to tinker with legal and institutional accomplishments of earlier periods, but it simply lacks the tools or the legitimacy to undertake any comprehensive efforts.

Second, the institutions that Fayyad can maintain are strictly administrative in nature. The Monetary Authority operates impressively, overseeing a banking system that has weathered innumerable storms. The Ministry of Education can continue examining students every year in the midst of political disruption and turmoil. And it can tinker with the curriculum developed in the 1990s—though too many changes risk furthering the divide between the West Bank and Gaza (because the educational system in Gaza is under Hamas's control).

These accomplishments are not small and I do not belittle them. But when the focus turns to the broader political context (elections, political parties) or society (NGOs [nongovernmental organizations], professional associations), Fayyad simply has no instruments at his disposal to stop or even slow the alarming decay.

Where Are the New Institutions?

Does it really matter that Fayyad is only improving existing institutions, rather than building new ones?

Not really, but understanding the history of Palestinian institutional development can help us project its current ills and likely course a bit more accurately.

Since Fayyad's cabinet was formed in 2007, there have been very few new institutions built, as I noted in the last paper. But the pre-existing nature of Palestinian institutions was simply not the source of my pessimism regarding Fayyadism or my criticism of the international reliance on Fayyadism. Instead, I claimed that a broader and long-term view of Palestinian institutions and their trajectory simply does not present a happy picture. While there has been limited progress in some institutions, others have undergone stark regression. The contrast I drew with the 1990s was to show how more institutional progress was made as a result of a messy political process with genuine democratic elements than with the current purely technocratic and authoritarian approach.

It was during the 1990s that ministries were built, comprehensive laws were written, a new curriculum devised, procedures designed, elections held, and regulations written. By the late 1990s, there were increasing signs of competence, participation by civic groups, and transparency. And there were gaping holes—international disinterest, presidential suspicions, Israeli contempt, and an overemphasis by almost all governments (Israeli, Palestinian, and American) on security.

In the previous paper, I focused on the areas of institutional development I am most familiar with (based on fifteen years of intermittent research on Palestinian politics) and compared the "state building" of the last few years—an antipolitical, authoritarian, and limited process—to that which took place during the Oslo period, when real institutions were built. The earlier process was messy, uneven, and deeply problematic as large parts of it were resisted by the then-Palestinian leader and sometimes undermined by the international community. But it was still a genuine political process and one that was therefore far more deeply rooted in society than the present antiseptic and technocratic effort.

One of the flaws of the earlier efforts—the emphasis on security in a manner that undermined the rule of law and undermined regime legitimacy—is actually being repeated today under international pressure.

Limited Reach

Is it accurate to say that Fayyadism is only limited to Ramallah? Isn't it more fair to acknowledge that he is trying to cover the entire West Bank?

Both statements are largely true. Fayyadism is most effective in Ramallah. But Fayyad's cabinet is trying desperately to extend its reach. That effort should be noted and probably deserves support. But it is inherently limited.

There is no doubt that Fayyad and his cabinet have launched a large number of local projects throughout the West Bank. I noted in my earlier paper how Fayyad has personally been visible outside of the major cities and how much of a departure this was from the behavior of previous officials.

The point can also be made more generally: Fayyad has placed the issue of Palestinian Authority jurisdiction over Area C back on the table, an impressive political accomplishment. The Oslo Accords divided up the West Bank into three areas. Area C—large in area but sparse in population—is often referred to as operating under total Israeli control. That is not supposed to be the case. Palestinians in Area C were to be governed by Palestinian civil institutions but security and some other areas were under Israeli control. In other words, Palestinian schoolchildren in Area C were to attend Palestinian schools run by the Palestinian Authority educational system, but no Palestinian police could operate there. (Area C was also supposed to diminish in size, but that process stopped over a decade ago.) That arrangement never worked well even when the Oslo process was at its height; since the beginning of the intifada [uprising] Palestinian Authority operations in Area C have suffered decay and neglect. Fayyad is trying to reverse that.

But as with Fayyadism generally, the new thrust in Area C might be laudable but cannot be seen as tantamount to state building. First, it is limited by the occupation: as others have noted, "Israel's control of Area C remains undisturbed." Second, it may deliver new school buildings and more wells, but it cannot deliver better politics: local elections were cancelled earlier this year by the same Fayyad cabinet that is promising better services.

Popular Support

If the programs are popular with the Palestinian people, doesn't that make Fayyadism democratic?

No. Such a claim is based on a misunderstanding of polls in general and of Palestinian poll results.

Palestinian political polls have risen in sophistication and provide valuable information, but they are a single (and sometimes volatile) measure of political dynamics. At present, Palestinian public opinion has not coalesced around any heroes (and provides evidence of increasing political alienation), but it is indisputable that Fayyad's standing has risen. And more broadly, he is treated with a bit more respect domestically and has discovered a political voice.

The problem with relying on polls is obvious: popularity in the polls can be ephemeral; it certainly does not deliver a mandate and can evaporate at a whiff of misstep or crisis. It certainly does not translate into an institution or state-building project. And the polls obscure the underlying problem that there is no organized political base for Fayyad's technocratic project.

The relationship between polls and institution building might best be seen by a reference to the local elections fiasco. These were abruptly cancelled earlier this year when Fatah proved so disorganized that it asked President [Mahmoud] Abbas to direct Fayyad's cabinet to cancel the call it had issued earlier. If standing in the polls translated into institutional strength, how was the prime minister and his cabinet so easily cowed? And had the elections not been cancelled, no Fayyadists would have won—because none were even running.

Alternatives

If Fayyadism is not building a state, what is the alternative?

My earlier paper was long on diagnosis and short on cure. And there is no easy alternative to the current policy. Indeed, I would not present any policy suggestions as an alternative in a literal sense: there is no reason to abandon current policies. But there is a desperate need to supplement them and stop the unpersuasive charade that they are sufficient in themselves to move toward a solution.

More specifically, I do not suggest that Fayyadism be abandoned (though the most obvious authoritarian practices such as illegal arrests and political purges pursued in the West Bank should probably be rethought immediately because of their high political costs). Nor do I suggest that Western support for Palestinian institution building be abandoned. Indeed, the sudden high-level U.S. attention to the details of Palestinian institutional development is a welcome departure from the [US president Bill] Clinton years (when there was a marked indifference at top levels) and the [US president George W.] Bush years (when senior leaders gave strong verbal but virtually no practical support outside of the security sector).

A variety of approaches are available. My Carnegie [Endowment for International Peace] colleague Michele Dunne has sketched out one that integrates Israeli-Palestinian diplomacy with attention to Palestinian politics. A year and a half ago [in early 2008], I offered a more radical proposal that involved postponing conflict-ending diplomacy but also called for far greater attention to Palestinian political realities. What we share is a belief that reviving Palestinian political life is vital to any attempt to resolve or even to manage the conflict. The existing approach, based on an assumption that a comprehensive Israeli-Palestinian agreement can be negotiated and then used as a device for ousting Hamas from control of Gaza is implausible. Yet it has been the basis of United States policy since 2007 and has been endorsed by Fayyad.

No mechanism has been publicly offered for reuniting the Palestinian Authority other than elections—which, given the current circumstances, are highly unlikely. Supporters of Fayyadism who decry the undemocratic actions of Hamas (on the plausible grounds that it seized power in Gaza and has blocked the work of the electoral commission) do not explain why they think Hamas could be convinced or coerced into allowing a referendum or national elections. And the actions of the Ramallah government (which showed little respect for the results of the 2006 elections, claimed constitutional authorities they clearly did not possess, decreed an electoral law that bars Hamas from running, and cancelled local elections for specious reasons) hardly give it the democratic high ground.

But if the present approach is unworkable, it is not clear that any quick fix will work. It must be frankly acknowledged that attention to Palestinian reconciliation would probably make progress on Israel–Palestinian negotiations impossible for the present. An approach that takes Palestinian politics seriously and prioritizes rather than postpones the issues of Gaza and Hamas would be difficult in its design, uncertain in its effectiveness, distasteful in its implications, and necessarily slow in its progress. But at least it would be grounded in the realities of today rather than pretending that the conditions of the 1990s—a viable peace process and a slowly emerging Palestinian polity—still obtain.

Recognizing Reality

If Fayyadism is limited in what it can accomplish, why has it generated so much support? Do international backers have a solid appreciation of the realities on the ground?

Most observers close to the ground—even those who are, like me, respectful of Fayyad personally—note the limitations of what his program has done and can accomplish. While I focused on law and education, those whose expertise lies in other areas report findings analogous to mine.

For instance, in the economic sphere, many observers note that the Fayyad cabinet has presided over impressive rates of growth but note deep structural problems (a reliance on foreign assistance, continued restrictions on mobility, general political fragility) that collectively suggest we are witnessing a partial recovery rather than the flourishing of sustainable long-term economic development. For instance, a recent report by the United Nations Conference on Trade and Development noted:

> The economy of the occupied Palestinian territory (oPt) continued to perform well below potential in 2009. There were signs of improvement in GDP [gross domestic product] growth and other indicators, but these need to be interpreted cautiously in view of the wider context. Territorial fragmentation, inequalities and welfare divergence continued to grow, aid dependence deepened, and access to natural and economic resources shrank. Private investment continued to be hampered by mobility restrictions and the risk of introducing new restrictions at any moment.

Similarly, the International Crisis Group focuses on the security sector and advances a respectful warning:

> The undeniable success of the reform agenda has been built in part on popular fatigue and despair—the sense that the situation had so deteriorated that Palestinians are prepared to swallow quite a bit for the sake of stability, including

deepened security cooperation with their foe. Yet, as the situation normalizes over time, they could show less indulgence. Should Israeli-Palestinian negotiations collapse—and, with them, any remaining hope for an agreement—Palestinian security forces might find it difficult to keep up their existing posture.

The reform agenda also was built on the intra-Palestinian split which, in the short term, has helped foster greater PA-IDF [Palestinian Authority–Israel Defense Forces] cooperation. Still, the intensity and scope of the anti-Hamas campaign carry many important consequences. They have undercut the PA's claim to be the true national authority, weakened President Abbas's mandate to speak in the name of all Palestinians and diminished prospects for reconciliation, thereby both complicating Israeli-Palestinian negotiations and enhancing Hamas's incentive to disrupt them. In the longer run, the split with Hamas and disregard for democratic norms are thus deeply at odds with the emergence of a strong, representative, legitimate national movement upon which Palestinians, but also Israelis, depend to achieve and sustain a historic peace agreement.

Yet if analysts and those on the ground recognize the limits of Fayyadism, there are many who are so invested in its success (and many as well who are invested in its failure) that they tend to read reality only through the lenses of their wishes. Those who warmly greeted my paper for their own political reasons ranged from settler blogs in the West Bank to the pro-Hamas Palestinian daily in Gaza—though the latter found no room in its summary for my description of Hamas as a "bloody-minded" movement. On the other hand, Fayyad himself dismissed it as "childish."

The paper generated a similar pattern of reactions from those in official positions in the United States, Europe, and Palestine (many of which were relayed to me indirectly). In general, mid-level analysts, officials, and observers in all three locations have come to conclusions similar to mine. But those at more senior levels, especially those most invested in the current policies, have reacted more negatively and viewed it as politically damaging. The fact that they have been made aware of the paper at all is perhaps evidence of the deep disquiet over the direction of policy in the middle and lower ranks.

Periodical and Internet Sources Bibliography

The following articles have been selected to supplement the diverse views presented in this chapter.

Peter Beinart	"Israeli-Palestinian Peace Talks Won't Solve the Jewish State Problem," Daily Beast, August 13, 2013. www.thedailybeast.com.
The Economist	"Reconciliation at Last?," December 8, 2012.
Robert Fantina	"Obama, Israel, and Palestine," *Counterpunch*, March 22–24, 2013.
Hassan Jabareen	"Why Palestinians Can't Recognize a 'Jewish State,'" *Haaretz* (Tel Aviv), September 2, 2011.
Yosef Kuperwasser and Shalom Lipner	"The Problem Is Palestinian Rejectionism," *Foreign Affairs*, November–December 2011.
Michael Lerner	"Recognize Palestine *and* Reaffirm Israel as a Jewish State," *Huffington Post*, September 14, 2011. www.huffingtonpost.com.
Joseph Levine	"On Questioning the Jewish State," *New York Times*, March 9, 2013.
Rachel Miller	"Why Israel Should Be a Jewish State," *Fort Lauderdale (FL) Sun-Sentinel*, August 24, 2011.
Joshua Mitnick	"Israeli-Palestinian Jolt? Why Some Want to Dismantle PA," *Christian Science Monitor*, November 15, 2011.
Daniel Pipes	"Obama to Palestinians: Accept the Jewish State," *National Review*, March 28, 2013.
Ben White	"Israel's Definition as a 'Jewish State,'" Al Jazeera, April 8, 2013. http://america.aljazeera.com.

Chapter 4

How Should the United States Treat the Palestinian Territories?

Chapter Preface

On July 29, 2013, direct negotiations commenced between Israeli and Palestinian diplomatic representatives in Washington, DC, to come up with a peaceful resolution to the conflict that has profoundly affected not only the Middle East but the entire world. Key to the renewal of peace talks were the efforts of the US secretary of state, John Kerry. For many observers, the hands-on role of the United States in initiating and monitoring peace negotiations was essential for keeping both Israel and the Palestinians on track and working toward the implementation of a two-state solution in the Middle East.

In his update on the negotiations, Secretary Kerry affirmed that the United States would continue to play a proactive role in implementing a two-state solution and establishing an independent Palestinian state. "The United States will work continuously with both parties as a facilitator every step of the way," he promised. "We all understand the goal that we're working towards: two states living side by side in peace and security. Two states because two proud peoples each deserve a country to call their own. Two states because the children of both peoples deserve the opportunity to realize their legitimate aspirations in security and in freedom. And two states because the time has come for a lasting peace."

Dr. Saeb Erekat, the Palestinian diplomatic envoy, concurred with Secretary Kerry's statement. "Palestinians have suffered enough, and no one benefits more from the success of this endeavor than Palestinians. I am delighted that all final status issues are on the table and will be resolved without any exceptions, and it's time for the Palestinian people to have an independent, sovereign state of their own. It's time for the Palestinians to live in peace, freedom, and dignity within their own independent, sovereign state."

The Israeli representative, minister of justice Tzipi Livni, commented on the promising opportunity that both countries had to forge a new peace agreement with the help of the United States. "A new opportunity is being created for us, for all of us, and we cannot afford to waste it," she asserted. "Now, I hope that our meeting today and the negotiations that we have re-launched . . . will cause . . . a spark of hope, even if it is small, to emerge out of [the] cynicism and pessimism that is so often heard. It is our task to work together so we can transform that spark of hope into something real and lasting."

Although some frustrated critics derided the peace negotiations as futile, many observers around the world viewed any attempt to address the complicated and deep-seated obstacles to peace in the region as a positive step. The role of the United States in the process is regarded as crucial to the renewal of Israeli-Palestinian talks and to the implementation of any agreement.

The US role in the peace process is one of the subjects debated in the following chapter, which explores the US treatment of the Palestinian Territories. Other viewpoints in the chapter examine the US attitude toward Palestinian statehood, US foreign aid to the Palestinian Authority, and the responsibility of the United States to stop Israeli human rights abuses in the region.

| "*[The United States] should at least recognize the [Palestinian] state.*"

The United States Should Recognize Palestinian Statehood

Zvi Bar'el

Zvi Bar'el is an educator, newspaper columnist, and the Middle East affairs analyst for the Israeli newspaper Haaretz. *In the following viewpoint, he urges the United States to recognize Palestinian statehood instead of opposing the resolution at the United Nations. Bar'el notes that the United States has already expressed its support of a Palestinian state, and Palestine has fulfilled all the threshold conditions. Casting a veto at the United Nations will hurt the United States more than the Palestinians, he argues; its opposition to the resolution has alienated it from its European allies, makes Israel look like a liar, and has led the United Nations to take a leadership role in the matter. The United States has no one to blame but itself for the quandary it finds itself in, the author contends, because it had the opportunity to negotiate Palestinian statehood earlier and thus avoid this diplomatic crisis.*

Zvi Bar'el, "US Should Recognize Palestinian State," *Haaretz*, September 21, 2011. Reproduced with permission.

As you read, consider the following questions:

1. What Palestinian leader does the author identify as being denied a US visa in 1998?

2. How many countries are members of the United Nations by Bar'el's count?

3. According to the author, what US diplomat had to announce the US veto of Palestinian statehood at the United Nations?

Memory is short and forgetfulness is often deliberate, but 23 years ago the UN General Assembly decided to move its session from New York to Switzerland so that Palestine Liberation Organization head Yasser Arafat could deliver a speech. The reason: U.S. Secretary of State George Schultz refused to issue Yasser Arafat an entry visa to the United States.

Today, too [in September 2011], with the opening of the session of the General Assembly, Washington is standing like a fortified wall blocking the entry of Palestine to the UN building. Although Palestinian Authority [PA] President Mahmoud Abbas has no problem getting a visa, when he comes to ask for a state for the Palestinians he is put on a roller coaster. The list of threats and future punishments to be imposed on him and his country, if it is established, guarantees that this will be a state that is battered from birth.

Here is colonialism in all its glory. After all, the United States agrees that there should be a Palestinian state, it even twisted the arm of Prime Minister Benjamin Netanyahu a little bit, cautiously so it wouldn't hurt, so that he would blurt out the necessary formula "two states for two peoples." U.S. President Barack Obama even spoke about the optimal borders of the Palestinian state and Abbas was not yet required to recognize Israel.

After all, Arafat already recognized it. Palestine fulfilled all the threshold conditions. And still, this state has only one chance of being born the American way—through negotiations that will lead to a consensual agreement and a handshake. And if Israel's hand is missing, never mind, the Palestinians will wait until it grows [back].

Key Lessons Learned

But Abbas has learned a thing or two from Israel. The main lesson he has learned is that his real negotiations are not with Israel but with Washington. The second lesson: The negotiations must not take place on a playing field that is convenient for Obama, but rather at the United Nations. There Obama is not facing a beggarly Palestinian Authority that can be frightened with a shout, but 193 countries, each of which must be negotiated with.

New York is not [the Palestinian capital city of] Ramallah. Abbas saw how Israel chose its own playing field in the U.S. Congress, and carefully responded in kind. Instead of going out on a limb, he planted the tree by himself, nurtured it, diligently recruited most of the countries in the world, was helped substantially by Israel's mistakes, took good advantage of Jerusalem's isolation, examined the pros and cons and decided that even in loss there would be great gain.

The U.S. Conundrum

If the United States casts a veto in the UN Security Council, it will cause more damage to Washington than to Abbas; if he makes do with recognition in the General Assembly, it will be in exchange for an American commitment to support a Palestinian state if negotiations fail, as they will.

Abbas caused Washington to be embroiled in a dispute with its European colleagues, and presented Israel as a cripple. He is forcing the United Nations to do what it usually fails to do: to find a peaceful solution to conflicts. As a bonus he caused Netanyahu to say that he is going to deliver a "speech of truth" at the United Nations, thereby admitting in effect that until now he has been lying.

Palestinian Statehood

On 29 November 2012, the United Nations General Assembly voted to recognize Palestine as a "non-member observer state." Palestine will now be able to join UN agencies, such as the International Criminal Court. While 138 members, including Russia, China, India, Brazil, and many Eurozone countries, voted for the resolution, nine countries, including Israel, the United States, and Canada, voted against the measure. Forty-one nations, including the United Kingdom and Germany, abstained from voting.

On 6 January 2013, Abbas told West Bank officials that the Palestinian Authority would begin labeling public documents with "State of Palestine," replacing the previous phrase "Palestinian Authority," due to the United Nations' decision to upgrade its status to a non-member observer state. Abbas said that stamping passports, identification cards, drivers' licenses, and the like with the new status will strengthen the Palestinian state "on the ground and build its institutions . . . and its sovereignty over its land."

Gale Cengage Learning,
Global Issues in Context Online Collection, *2013.*

The panic in Washington is genuine. It was evident when David Hale, Obama's special envoy, was unable to control his temper and simply shouted at Abbas when he understood that he had no intention of retreating from his initiative.

Anger and helplessness could also be detected in the voice of U.S. Secretary of State Hillary Clinton, when she announced that the United States would cast a veto in the Security Council. Suddenly she realized that the Israeli-Palestinian conflict is not only "the business of the parties involved" but threatens Washington's regional and international status.

A Lost Opportunity

If the United States fails to recognize the Palestinian state, it will have difficulty sidelining its rivals in the new Middle East, where the public has more power than the rulers; if it recognizes the Palestinian state, it will have to ensure its sustainability, in other words, to direct the sanctions against Israel. Truly a bad situation for a great power that aspires to draw the map of the new Middle East.

Had it only made an effort to achieve genuine negotiations when that was still possible, had it invested its efforts into reaching an agreement that it is now investing in preventing the declaration of independence, had it shared the threats equally between the PA and Israel, it may not have found itself in this difficult situation.

It should at least recognize the state now. It should recall what has happened since it refused to grant Arafat his visa.

"If the president chooses to stand by and let a resolution [granting Palestinian statehood] happen, . . . the proper U.S. response is to ignore whatever passes."

The United States Should Not Recognize Palestinian Statehood

John R. Bolton

John R. Bolton is a senior fellow at the American Enterprise Institute and the former US representative to the United Nations. In the following viewpoint, he finds it crucial that the United States oppose the granting of Palestinian statehood at the United Nations General Assembly. Bolton argues that the UN does not have the authority to declare statehood. Furthermore, discussion of the resolution should be held by the Security Council, not the General Assembly. If a resolution does pass, Bolton contends that the US should just ignore it and consider cutting off funding to the UN. He suggests that even holding the vote on the resolution damages Israel's legitimacy and security as well as the credibility of the United Nations.

As you read, consider the following questions:

1. How many member states does Bolton predict will vote in favor of Palestinian statehood at the United Nations General Assembly in 2011?

2. In the author's opinion, why should General Assembly Resolution 181 not be used to justify the creation of a Palestinian state?

3. In what year does Bolton say that the General Assembly adopted the infamous "Zionism is racism" resolution?

An aversion to reality can be a powerfully destructive force. Its most visible manifestation in international affairs lies in trying to create political "facts on the ground" through the United Nations. Accordingly, it is no surprise that the Middle East, one of our most intractable problems, provokes so much U.N. activity, even though the real-world consequences are so limited.

The next episode of reality avoidance is the near certainty that, this fall [in 2011], the General Assembly will vote to recognize a Palestinian state, possibly also declaring that state's borders with Israel to be the 1967 lines (actually, just the Green Line marking the 1949 cease-fire positions). Absent dramatic action by Washington, perhaps 150 or more of the U.N.'s 192 members, including many nominal U.S. allies, will vote in favor.

Will such a resolution actually make any difference? Is it political theater, or something to take seriously? While a General Assembly convulsion would be largely symbolic, symbols can have consequences if you accept their underlying mythology. How will Israel respond? How should the United States respond?

Some Considerations

First, neither the Security Council nor the General Assembly has the legal authority to declare statehood. The U.N.'s website says candidly that the world body "does not possess any authority to recognize either a state or a government." Attempting to ram such a declaration through is not merely improper but destructive of the U.N. itself.

Some, however, argue that there is precedent, citing General Assembly Resolution 181 of 1947, which endorsed a plan to partition the former British League of Nations mandate into Jewish and Arab states, and a "special international regime" for Jerusalem. They should read what the resolution actually says. Like all assembly resolutions, it is not legally binding. It simply "recommends" the partition plan in question, and "requests that the Security Council take the necessary measures" to implement it. The council never adopted the plan. Although the Jewish leadership accepted it, the Arabs did not, and a multi-front Arab assault followed. End of precedent.

While the foregoing international law arguments are complex and probably have eternal life, they will settle nothing today. Perhaps the most reality-averse idea of all is believing the League of Nations' or the U.N.'s actions more than 50 years ago reveal a solution for today. Resolving the Arab-Israeli dispute is ultimately a matter of power and political resolve now, not ambiguous precedents and musty resolutions. If dust-gathering texts from the past could determine the outcome now, what logic requires us to go back merely a few decades? Why not go back millenniums for even more compelling authority?

United Nations Politics

Second, whatever serious political work is done at the U.N. is done by the Security Council, where the veto of the five permanent members—the United States, France, China, Britain and Russia—gives them predominance. For decades, this has aggravated Third World nations, the largest of which alternate between advocating the abolition of the veto or themselves becoming permanent members. If the U.N. is ever to play a constructive role in the Arab-Israeli dispute, it will be through the Security Council, not the General Assembly.

The council and the assembly jointly decide on the admission of new members to the U.N. Because the U.N. Charter provides that only "states" can be members, a decision to admit "Palestine" would obviously mean that those supporting membership considered "Palestine" to meet the charter's statehood requirement. Last year [2010], many believed the [Barack] Obama administration might not veto a Palestinian membership application, and the original Palestinian strategy was indeed to convene the council to seek U.N. admission, or at least declare a Palestinian state. The outcry from President Obama's political opponents, and even from otherwise supportive Democrats, punctured that balloon, thereby prompting statehood advocates' switch to the General Assembly's almost uniformly anti-Israel, anti-U.S. majority. This is the true indicator of reality aversion.

The Role of President Obama

Finally, if the president chooses to stand by and let a resolution happen, rather than taking dramatic diplomatic action such as threatening to cut off U.S. contributions to the U.N., the proper U.S. response is to ignore whatever passes. When the General Assembly adopted the infamous "Zionism is racism" resolution in 1975, Ambassador Daniel Patrick Moynihan responded: "The United States rises to declare that it does not acknowledge, that it will not abide by and that it will never acquiesce in this infamous act." That's a good place to start here as well. We should simply disregard the outcome, and tell the world so at every opportunity. Israel and whoever else stands tall and votes against the resolution in that very lonely General Assembly room should do the same.

The reality is that the controlling U.N. approach to this dispute is grounded in the decisions made after the 1967 and

1973 Arab-Israeli wars, namely Security Council Resolutions 242 and 338. These "land for peace" resolutions make no mention of "the 1967 borders" or any other specific line, and for very compelling reasons. Those who drafted these texts understood full well that the 1967 lines could never meet Israel's legitimate quest, in 242's words, "to live in peace within secure and recognized boundaries free from threats or acts of force." It has been America's consistent policy to support those Israeli aspirations, and should remain so today.

The Consequences of a UN Vote

Taking assembly recommendations to heart can only cause problems. True, a massive majority supporting Palestinian statehood will constitute yet another assault on Israel's legitimacy and its security needs. And while that vote is likely to be frustrating and bitter, it is best to treat it like the grass we tread beneath our feet.

In fact, a Palestinian statehood resolution will almost certainly wound the United Nations, perhaps gravely, just as for many Americans "Zionism is racism" delegitimized not Israel but the U.N. itself. Perhaps that risk will awaken our excessively multilateralist administration to the dangers of acquiescing in the Palestinian proposal. Does Obama believe that further discrediting the U.N. is really in our interest?

If, however, he continues to be the most anti-Israel president since 1948, then others will have to act. Congress could adopt legislation cutting off American contributions to the U.N. if the Palestinian resolution is adopted, which might persuade statehood advocates to back down. In any event, there will be fireworks this autumn over Turtle Bay [in New York], but no real harm as long as we remember that, in the end, it's just entertainment.

"U.S. aid to the Palestinian Authority should be closely tied to its compliance with previous agreements to fight terrorism, halt incitement against Israel, and negotiate a final peace settlement."

The United States Should Rethink Aid to the Palestinian Authority

James Phillips

James Phillips is the Senior Research Fellow for Middle Eastern Affairs at The Heritage Foundation in Washington, DC. In the following viewpoint, taken from his testimony before the Foreign Affairs Committee, he argues that the United States should block any effort to establish a Palestinian state that sponsors terrorism or tries to exploit anti-Israeli sentiment at the United Nations General Assembly to undermine Israeli security. Phillips contends that the United States should reexamine its commitment to aid to the Palestinian Authority and maintains that such aid should be "closely tied to its compliance with previous agreements to fight terrorism, halt incitement against Israel, and negotiate a fi-

James Phillips, "Promoting Peace? Reexamining Aid to the Palestinian Authority, Part II," The Heritage Foundation, September 14, 2011. Copyright © 2011 by James Phillips. All rights reserved. Reproduced with permission.

nal peace settlement." In the author's opinion, US aid should be leveraged to convince Palestinians that direct negotiations with Israel is the only way to achieve a Palestinian state.

As you read, consider the following questions:

1. According to Phillips, how much US aid has been showered on the Palestinians since the signing of the Oslo accords in 1993?

2. In what year does the Palestine Liberation Organization claim the establishment of a Palestinian state, according to Phillips?

3. What important statement about Palestinian statehood does the author say was made during the September 7, 2011, confirmation hearing of Wendy Sherman, the nominee for undersecretary of state?

My name is James Phillips, and I am the Senior Research Fellow for Middle Eastern Affairs at The Heritage Foundation. The views I express in this testimony are my own and should not be construed as representing any official position of The Heritage Foundation.

Since the signing of the 1993 Oslo peace accords, the U.S. has showered over $4 billion in bilateral aid on the Palestinians, who are one of the world's largest per capita recipients of international foreign aid. From FY [fiscal year] 2008 until this year [2011], annual U.S. bilateral aid to the West Bank and Gaza has averaged over $600 million, according to the Congressional Research Service. In FY 2011, this bilateral aid is set at $550 million, including $400 million in Economic Support Funds and $150 million for training and equipping Palestinian Authority security forces.

U.S. aid to the Palestinians is aimed at supporting Israeli-Palestinian peace negotiations; strengthening and reforming the Palestinian Authority, which was created through those negotiations; and improving the living standards of Palestinians to demonstrate the benefits of peaceful coexistence with Israel.

These are laudable goals, but unfortunately, peace negotiations have bogged down. Even worse, the Palestinian Authority has reached a rapprochement with Hamas, the Islamist extremist organization with a long record of terrorism, which not only is opposed to peace negotiations with Israel, but remains implacably committed to Israel's destruction.

The Palestinian Authority's relationship with Hamas and its ongoing efforts to include Hamas in a ruling coalition under a May 2011 power-sharing agreement raise disturbing questions about the long-term intentions of the Palestinian Authority and casts doubt on its commitment to negotiate a genuine peace with Israel. By consorting with Hamas terrorists, the Palestinian Authority is violating the Oslo accords and destroying the rationale for continued American aid.

The Issue of Palestinian Statehood

Palestinian leader Mahmoud Abbas also has chosen to pursue a dubious dead-end path to Palestinian statehood through the United Nations rather than through negotiations with Israel. This U.N. diplomatic gambit could derail any hope of resuming Israeli-Palestinian peace negotiations in the future and could destabilize the region by exacerbating the already tense atmosphere of Israeli-Palestinian relations and provoking widespread anti-Israel demonstrations that easily could spin out of control.

Palestinian leaders have called for popular demonstrations in support of their U.N. statehood campaign on September 20, and President Abbas is slated to address the U.N. General Assembly on September 21. Although the precise text of what the Palestinians will demand at the U.N. has not been divulged, it is expected to request U.N. endorsement for unilateral Palestinian statehood and the elevation of the Palestinian delegation to the status of a U.N. member state.

The Palestine Liberation Organization (PLO), the dominant organization within the Palestine Authority, has enjoyed observer status in the General Assembly since 1974. This entitles it to a seat in the General Assembly and allows it to speak at meetings, but it cannot vote. In 1988, the PLO delegation was formally designated "Palestine" under the terms of General Assembly Resolution 43/177, which acknowledged the Palestinian declaration of statehood in November 2008 and granted the delegation the privilege of having its communications issued and circulated as official U.N. documents.

If the Palestinian statehood gambit is blocked at the Security Council as expected, the Palestinians will push for formal General Assembly recognition of Palestine as a state and added rhetorical support for that claim through the elevation of the status of the Palestinian delegation from a non-voting observer "entity" to that of a non-member state observer. A large majority of the General Assembly's 193 member states are likely to support the Palestinians' unilateral statehood agenda, consistent with that body's long-standing anti-Israel bias. As Ambassador Dore Gold, Israel's former U.N. ambassador, has noted, "If there was a resolution whose first clause was anti-Israel and whose second clause was that the earth was flat, it would pass."

But the General Assembly has no authority to unilaterally grant full U.N. membership. It cannot override the U.N. Charter, which specifically requires a Security Council recommendation before admitting a new member state. Moreover, the U.N. role in state recognition is nonexistent beyond being a reflection of the sovereign decisions of the member states, and General Assembly resolutions are not legally binding on U.N. members.

Thus, a General Assembly vote on the issue, absent a Security Council recommendation, is merely symbolic. But it is a dangerous symbolism insofar as it convinces Palestinians that they need not negotiate with Israel and can instead achieve their goals unilaterally.

Consequences of Palestinian Statehood

The Palestinian delegation would undoubtedly exploit their enhanced status in the General Assembly as a "non-member state" observer to argue that Palestine is a sovereign state. Such enhanced status would better enable the Palestinian Authority to gain greater latitude in harnessing the U.N. machinery to launch spurious diplomatic, political, and quasi-legal challenges to Israel. For example, the Palestinian delegation would use this argument to bolster its efforts to gain membership in other U.N. bodies and organizations or use its new status as evidence of its right as a "sovereign state" to invite the International Criminal Court to investigate alleged crimes committed by Israel in the West Bank or Gaza.

In addition, a pro-statehood vote in the U.N. General Assembly could destabilize the region by giving cover to anti-Israel forces bent on the destruction of the Jewish state, undermining peace efforts, and triggering a downward spiral in Israeli–Palestinian relations by inflaming Palestinian demonstrations that could easily degenerate into violent clashes.

The PLO already claims that it established a "state" in 1988, so it would appear that it has little to gain in its current statehood campaign except for greater leverage to undermine Israel's perceived legitimacy at the U.N. Israel has been a U.N. member state since 1949 and in fact was established after the U.N. endorsed the partition of the British Mandate for Palestine, which Israel accepted but the Arab states rejected, opting instead to attempt to invade and destroy Israel. To ignore the U.N.'s initial support for Israel's creation and to permit the body to be co-opted in a politicized effort to delegitimize Israel at the behest of an organization that is partnered with a terrorist group would turn the U.N.'s founding principles upside down.

The Palestinian push for unilateral statehood also will deal a major setback to Israeli-Palestinian peace prospects. Such a unilateral move by the Palestinian Authority would violate previous Israeli-Palestinian peace accords, amplify Israeli concerns about Palestinian abandonment of diplomatic commitments, and discourage Palestinians from making the hard compromises necessary to negotiate a genuine and lasting peace.

The Oslo Accords

The Palestinians' unilateral statehood gambit is a breach of the Oslo accords, which bar both parties from unilaterally changing the status of the West Bank and Gaza. A unilateral declaration of statehood would also undermine all internationally accepted frameworks for peace, including past U.N. peace efforts. It would violate U.N. Security Council Resolution 242 and the U.N.-sponsored Road Map for Peace, as well as other U.N. statements that call for the creation of a Palestinian state and delineation of borders through a negotiated mutual agreement, not through unilateral declarations.

An endorsement of Palestinian statehood by the General Assembly would compound the negative impact on peace prospects by reinforcing the Palestinians' maximal demands for territory and short-circuiting possible future negotiations on this issue. The text of the resolution is expected to endorse Palestinian demands for a return to Israel's pre-1967 "borders" (in reality, the 1949 armistice lines). This will make it much harder for Palestinian leaders to compromise on this issue in the future, an outcome that is likely to derail peace negotiations because no Israeli government would accept a return to what former Israeli Foreign Minister Abba Eban derided as "Auschwitz lines."

Recent Historical Background on US Aid to the Palestinians

Since the establishment of limited Palestinian self-rule in the West Bank and Gaza Strip in the mid-1990s, the U.S. government has committed more than $4 billion in bilateral assistance to the Palestinians in the West Bank and Gaza, who are among the largest per capita recipients of foreign aid worldwide . . . .

Following the death of Yasser Arafat in 2004 and his succession by Mahmoud Abbas as PA president in 2005, Congress and the [George W.] Bush Administration increased U.S. assistance to the Palestinians. However, after the 2006 Hamas victory in Palestinian Legislative Council elections. . . . The United States halted direct foreign aid to the PA but continued providing humanitarian and project assistance to the Palestinian people through international and NGOs [nongovernmental organizations]. The ban on direct assistance continued during the brief tenure of a Hamas-led power-sharing government (February to June 2007) . . . .

Subsequent events altered the situation dramatically. In June 2007, Hamas forcibly took control of the Gaza Strip. PA President and Fatah head Mahmoud Abbas, calling the move a "coup," dissolved the power-sharing government and tasked the politically independent technocrat Salam Fayyad to serve as prime minister and organize a new PA "caretaker" government in the West Bank. Within days, the United States lifted its economic and political embargo on the PA.

Jim Zanotti,
Congressional Research Service,
January 18, 2013.

The unilateral Palestinian push for statehood violates not only previous Palestinian agreements with Israel, but also those with the United States, which was a co-signatory of the Oslo accords. Yet the [Barack] Obama Administration has bent over backwards to avoid criticizing the Palestinian Authority. President Obama made it clear that the U.N. was not an appropriate venue for addressing the statehood issue in his May 19 speech on Middle East policy, but he stopped short of threatening a veto. It was not until the September 7 confirmation hearing of Wendy Sherman, the Administration's nominee for the post of Undersecretary of State, that an Administration official publicly and unequivocally stated that the Administration would use the veto, and this came only in response to a question.

The U.S. Role

This low-key, reticent approach has failed to halt the Palestinian U.N. drive for unilateral statehood. It is long past time for the Obama Administration to become proactively engaged on this issue at the highest levels. Secretary of State [Hillary] Clinton, and the President himself, should explicitly and forcefully state American opposition to Palestinian plans to seek statehood through unilateral action rather than through bilateral negotiations with Israel. They should explicitly state that the U.S. will veto any Security Council resolution recognizing Palestinian statehood or calling for full membership in the U.N. before an Israeli-Palestinian peace agreement is concluded.

The only legitimate route to Palestinian statehood is through bilateral Israeli-Palestinian negotiations. Yet Palestinian Authority President Mahmoud Abbas has permitted only two weeks of negotiations during September 2010 since the beginning of the Obama Administration. Washington should press Abbas to drop his refusal to negotiate unless Jerusalem first meets his demand for a settlement freeze. This demand, unfortunately encouraged by the Obama Administration's own shortsighted focus on settlements during its early months, is not supported by the terms of the Oslo accords.

The United States should also declare that it will withhold voluntary or assessed funds from any U.N. organization that admits Palestine as a state or grants it non-member state observer status.

In 1989, after the PLO issued its first "declaration of statehood" and sought to gain membership in U.N. organizations, such as the World Health Organization, to bolster their claims of statehood, the first Bush Administration [i.e., George H.W. Bush] blocked this effort by threatening to withhold U.S. funding for the United Nations. Secretary of State James Baker publicly warned that the U.S. would cut funding to any international organization which made changes in the PLO's status as an observer organization.

While the Obama Administration's deference to the United Nations and its "lead from behind" proclivities make such a strong stand unlikely, Congress can step into the breach and pass legislation prohibiting funding to any U.N. organization that endorses unilateral Palestinian statehood, admits Palestine as a member state, or grants it non-member state observer status.

Cutting U.S. Aid

Congress should also cut U.S. economic aid to the Palestinian Authority if it continues to shun negotiations with Israel and ignore its commitments under previous agreements. U.S. aid is not an entitlement and should be closely tied to the Palestinian Authority's performance in demonstrating its commitment to peace.

If Palestinians persist in their efforts to sidestep direct negotiations with Israel in favor of some form of illusory "statehood," then they should expect to look elsewhere for funds to build that pseudo-state. The Palestinian Authority recently announced that it will pay only half wages to its employees in September, the second time in three months that it has been forced to cut pay, because of a huge shortfall in funding pledges from Arab states. This could lead Palestinian leaders to think twice before putting their financial future in the hands of unreliable Arab governments who are more interested in using the Palestinian issue as a means of attacking Israel than they are interested in building a Palestinian state.

I would recommend that U.S. aid for Palestinian security forces be continued only if the Israeli government certifies that those security forces continue to play a positive role in fighting terrorism in compliance with the Palestinians' Oslo commitments. Bilateral security cooperation between Israeli and Palestinian Authority security forces reportedly has been improved in recent years despite continued strains between the political leaderships. The Palestinian Authority security forces could still play a valuable role in maintaining public order during the impending Palestinian demonstrations and combating Hamas terrorists in the West Bank. But if the Palestinian Authority implements its power-sharing agreement with Hamas and forms a joint government, then this security aid also must be ended, by law, to prevent U.S. funds from being diverted to terrorists.

The bottom line is that the United States must block any effort to create a Palestinian state that sponsors terrorism or seeks to make an end run around negotiations with Israel by exploiting the anti-Israeli bias of the U.N. General Assembly. U.S. aid to the Palestinian Authority should be closely tied to its compliance with previous agreements to fight terrorism, halt incitement against Israel, and negotiate a final peace settlement. The United States should leverage its aid to convince Palestinians that the only realistic path to a Palestinian state is through direct negotiations leading to a peace treaty with Israel.

> *"Given the amounts [Congress has] over time authorized for the Palestinians, [it has] the absolute right to demand . . . far more US government pressure to stop the corruption [in the Palestinian Authority]."*

The United States Should Make a Concerted Effort to Root Out Corruption in the Palestinian Authority

Elliot Abrams

Elliot Abrams is the Senior Fellow for Middle Eastern Studies at the Council on Foreign Affairs and former foreign policy adviser to US presidents Ronald Reagan and George W. Bush. In the following viewpoint, taken from congressional testimony, he maintains that although a reexamination of US aid to the Palestinian Authority (PA) is necessary in light of the push toward Palestinian statehood, cutting aid altogether would make things harder for both Israelis and Palestinians. Abrams recommends that the United States wait and see what the Palestine Liberation Organization (PLO) does after the vote on a United Nations resolu-

tion on Palestinian statehood in September 2011. If it is clear that the PLO is uninterested in moving forward to negotiate for peace with the Israelis, then the United States should close the PLO office in Washington, cut aid to the United Nations Relief and Works Agency for Palestine Refugees in the Near East (UNRWA), and take a tougher line on PA and PLO corruption, Abrams argues. It is perfectly reasonable to demand a better accounting of how US aid is spent in the Palestinian territories, he asserts.

As you read, consider the following questions:

1. According to Abrams, what infamous twentieth-century tyrant did Haj Amin al-Husseini lead the Palestinians to support?

2. When did the US government first grant a waiver to keep the Palestine Liberation Organization (PLO) office in Washington open, according to the author?

3. How many Palestinian refugees does Abrams say are eligible for the services of the United Nations Relief and Works Agency for Palestine Refugees (UNRWA)?

A id to the PA [Palestinian Authority] has been extended in the hope that we are ... promoting peace. Certainly in the years since the death of [Palestinian leader] Yasser Arafat our aid has done so. We have helped promote Israeli-Palestinian cooperation, and helped Palestinians who would rather build up their own state than curse their neighbor. I could spend a good deal of time listing the many achievements of our aid programs and the good they have done, both directly and by supporting the PA's positive efforts once real reform began.

Reexamining US Aid to the Palestinians

There are reasons, however, to take another look at the program, and obviously one of them is the coming UN vote on

Palestinian statehood. That maneuver in New York by the PLO [Palestine Liberation Organization] leadership suggests that they are turning away from both direct negotiations with Israel and from state-building at home and toward confrontational melodramas in Turtle Bay [the area of New York where the UN is located]. The United States has been trying to get the Palestinians to the negotiating table for over two years now without success. But President Abbas instead seems determined to do something entirely different: he seems most concerned about his legacy. Today he is the man who lost Gaza. So he wants a UN declaration about Palestinian statehood, and he wants his unity deal with Hamas, and then presumably he thinks he can leave the scene saying there is national unity and progress toward statehood. This is a disastrous course for the Palestinian people. Like Haj Amin al-Husseini, who led the Palestinians in the first half of the twentieth century into support for Hitler, and Yasser Arafat, who in the second half led them into terrorism, he will be going down a dark alley.

You therefore face a real problem: what is to be done about our aid program if the PLO leadership, which is also the Fatah Party leadership, insists on going forward against all American advice? What should change if the PLO insists on getting itself declared a non-member observer state by the General Assembly?

First I would respond that something must. Members of Congress have warned against this step in New York and said there would be consequences, and you should be as good as your word.

Second I would say the best response is not to zero out all aid to the PA. Some programs are very much in our own interest and Israel's, such as the security programs. Defunding them right now would make life harder for Israelis and Palestinians alike. Nor do I favor generally cutting off the PA, for several reasons. The entire PA (as opposed to the Fatah and

PLO leadership) is not to blame for what the PLO/Fatah crew is planning in New York. A collapse of the PA would not be in our interest nor in Israel's or for that matter Jordan's. In fact it might benefit only Hamas and other extremist and terrorist groups.

So what actions might you take, then, that are in my view better responses?

I have four suggestions.

A Wait-and-See Approach

First, wait and see what Abbas and the PLO top brass do in and after the vote. Do they go to the Security Council to force an American veto? If so they will be deliberately seeking a confrontation with the United States and deliberately making things difficult for us in the region. Then there is the language of the resolution they put forward: is it as limited as possible, or do they seek to have the General Assembly pronounce on issues like borders and refugees and Jerusalem? If they do the latter they largely foreclose the chances for negotiations, for how will any Palestinian leader be able to accept less when he sits down with Israel than he has already gotten at the UN?

And what happens after the vote? If they then say, well now we have our symbolic victory and now we want to go to negotiations, without preconditions, obviously that positive move should be met with approval. It is more likely to happen if they know you are waiting and watching. On the other hand if they move immediately to create large and dangerous demonstrations, and immediately rush off to the International Criminal Court to demand prosecutions of Israeli officials, it will be obvious that they want confrontation not peace. And they should know what that means for aid levels. But keeping some of your powder dry is probably a good idea.

Then there is Hamas. You have said aid would be ended if they really consummate a unity deal with Hamas. If all aid has already been ended, that pressure point will be removed. It's another reason to allow some aid flows to continue until we see what game the PLO leaders are really playing.

Close the PLO Office

Second, I urge you to move after the vote to close the PLO office in Washington. Right now it operates under a presidential waiver of the 1987 law that ordered it closed, a waiver that has been granted every six months for decades. A waiver is necessary because of the PLO's long involvement in terrorism under Arafat. Close that office. The logic is that if the PLO has rejected American advice and insisted on the UN declaring it a state, then there is no need to allow the PLO to continue here. The PLO leadership will be saying it wishes to disappear, so let's cooperate and allow them to do so here in our capital.

End Aid to UNRWA

Third, start ending our aid to UNRWA. As you know, the world was awash in refugees after the Second World War and all of those refugees have been settled and absorbed—except the Palestinians. While Israel happily took in Jewish refugees from all over the world, and not least the Arab world, Arab countries continue to keep Palestinians in refugee status without citizenship or rights. UNRWA helps perpetuate this calamity. Every other group of refugees is handled by the UN-HCR, the UN High Commissioner for Refugees. UNHCR says its objective for refugees is as follows: "our ultimate goal is to help find durable solutions that will allow them to rebuild their lives in dignity and peace. There are three solutions open to refugees where UNHCR can help: voluntary repatriation; local integration; or resettlement to a third country in situations where it is impossible for a person to go back home or remain in the host country."

Compare what UNRWA says: "UNRWA (the United Nations Relief and Works Agency for Palestine Refugees in the Near East) provides assistance, protection and advocacy for

The World's Perspective on Yasser Arafat

To the end of his life, Arafat remained a polarizing figure. To most Palestinians, he remained *al-Khityar* (the old man), the almost mythical symbol of their drive for independence and dignity, who pulled together a dispersed and downtrodden people, turned them into a movement, and led them to the doorway of independence. To other Palestinians, he was a sell-out who bargained away cherished national rights in return for the illusion of independence. To many Arab leaders he was a nuisance at best and an enemy at worst, someone who symbolized the instability generated by the presence of millions of Palestinian refugees in their countries anxious for their own independent state.

Globally, Arafat generally was seen as a statesman from the developing world who, like so many others, started out as a fighter in the struggle for independence only to turn in the end to diplomacy. In 1994, he won the Nobel Peace Prize along with [Israeli prime minister Yitzhak] Rabin and Israeli Foreign Minister Shimon Peres as a result of their actions in bringing about the Oslo Accord. However, many Western countries in particular viewed him with considerable suspicion. Particularly in the United States and Israel, Arafat was vilified as the leader of an organization that first brought terrorist acts such as airplane hijackings to the Middle East. Israelis in particular vehemently demonized him as a deceitful terrorist, both before and after the Oslo peace process of the mid-1990s when they briefly had considered him a "partner for peace."

Gale Cengage Learning,
Biography in Context Online Collection, *2013.*

some 5 million registered Palestine refugees in Jordan, Lebanon, Syria and the occupied Palestinian territory, pending a solution to their plight." Pending a solution—in other words, it does nothing to advance the solution and instead perpetuates refugee status forever. For UNRWA adds this note: "The descendants of the original Palestine refugees are also eligible for registration. When the Agency started working in 1950, it was responding to the needs of about 750,000 Palestine refugees. Today, 5 million Palestine refugees are eligible for UNRWA services." So every other refugee problem has diminished over time; only in the case of UNRWA and the Palestinians does it grow, automatically, year after year. And we are complicit in that undertaking.

I realize that this hearing is predominantly about aid to the PA, but that aid comes in a context—and the context is a UN agency perpetuating the refugee problem forever. So UNRWA is my third point.

Address Corruption Problem

Fourth, take a far tougher line on PA and PLO corruption. I have the highest regard for Prime Minister Fayyad and I believe he is a completely honest official, so this is not a criticism of him. But he is surrounded by a Fatah/PLO crew that was thoroughly corrupt when Arafat was alive and I do not believe they have eliminated corruption since. In fact, since 2006 the very large Palestine Investment Fund or PIF has been out of Fayyad's control, and there are plenty of allegations about corruption in its activities and about self-dealing by its board. You don't have to spend much time in [the Palestinian capital city of] Ramallah to hear more allegations about growing corruption at the highest levels.

Given the amounts you have over time authorized for the Palestinians, you have the absolute right to demand better accounting, an investigation of the PIF, and far more U.S. government pressure to stop the corruption U.S. officials will privately acknowledge exists. It is a good way of telling the PLO officials that their caper in New York was a serious mistake and that they will pay a price for it.

Madam Chairman, you face a difficult set of issues here. All of us want an Israeli-Palestinian peace and want the Palestinians to be able to build up the institutions they will someday need to establish a decent and democratic state. Our aid programs help in that work. Ending them can set back those efforts. But the PLO leadership should know that if they turn from that work and from genuine negotiations with Israel, you are determined that they will pay the price. And in that determination, you are right.

| *"The Israeli-Palestinian conflict cannot be resolved without the direct and active involvement of the United States."*

The United States Should Take a More Proactive and Aggressive Role in Palestinian-Israeli Peace Talks

Alon Ben-Meir

Alon Ben-Meir is a journalist, author, and professor of international relations and Middle East Studies at New York University. In the following viewpoint, he regards the direct and active involvement of the United States to be integral to any resolution of the Israeli-Palestinian conflict and urges US diplomatic officials to take a more proactive role in bringing about meaningful negotiations between the two countries. Ben-Meir lists the priorities for the US president: visiting Israel and Palestine and restating the US commitment to a two-state solution; offering a general framework for negotiations; appointing an internationally recognized special envoy to move the negotiation process forward; reaching out to other Arab and Muslim states; and jumpstarting the Arab Peace Initiative (API). Resolving the Israeli-Palestinian conflict should be a top priority of any American administration because it is within US self-interest and the United States is in a unique position to make a meaningful difference in the peace process, Ben-Meir maintains.

As you read, consider the following questions:

1. According to the author, what were the bewildering comments made by US presidential candidate Mitt Romney about the Palestinians?

2. Who did President Barack Obama appoint to be a special envoy for Middle East peace only two days after the president's inauguration, according to Ben-Meir?

3. What leading Muslim states does the author suggest the United States reach out to in order to exert pressure on the Palestinians?

The Israeli-Palestinian conflict cannot be resolved without the direct and active involvement of the United States, using both inducements and coercive diplomacy to bring about a peaceful solution. If the conflict remains unresolved over the next couple of years it will most likely precipitate a massive violent conflagration to the detriment of the Israelis and Palestinians, and will also severely damage the U.S.' security, economic interests and its credibility in the region. For these reasons, what the next president of the U.S. does within a few months after his inauguration will determine the future prospect of a solution, and the extent to which the candidates adhere to their campaign rhetoric will have a clear and immediate effect on how the Israelis and Palestinians react to any new American initiative to resolve the conflict.

Mitt Romney's Position

Mitt Romney's position toward the conflict raises serious questions, not only about his timidity but also about his short-sightedness in connection with a complex conflict that has been simmering for decades and will, without a doubt, explode if a resolution is not found soon. In a number of bewildering statements, Romney blamed Palestinian "culture" as the cause of their current predicaments and faulted them for having "no interest whatsoever in establishing peace." With these comments, Romney is, in fact, sending the Israelis a clear message that they should maintain the occupation, further expand the settlements and keep the blockade on Gaza, while inferring that the U.S. will not bother to interfere. Conversely, Romney's message to the Palestinians is that they have missed many opportunities in the past to achieve peace, their yearning for statehood is a pipe dream and they should expect little, if any, assistance from a Romney administration.

In the wake of the Arab Spring, however, as the Palestinians watch young men and women in several Arab states fighting and dying for their freedoms, their own relative passivity at the present will not last forever. Romney's preference of "[kicking] the ball down the field," (that is, letting events take their own course) is dangerously misguided and ultimately detrimental to the cause of peace.

Indeed, should Romney become President and move to translate his campaign rhetoric into policy, he will seriously endanger Israel's very existence, which he presumably wishes to protect, and will compromise its future as an independent, democratic Jewish state while contributing to its isolation from the international community. At the same time, he will encourage the Palestinians to rise up out of desperation and hopelessness to end the occupation at whatever cost, akin to the rise of Arab youth against their own governments who are prepared to die for their freedom.

President Obama's Position

President Obama himself has contributed to the current impasse in part by insisting early in 2009 that the peace negotiations should start by first freezing the settlements, which was a nonstarter for the [Israeli prime minister Benjamin] Netanyahu government, and by failing to visit Israel when he travelled three times overseas, visiting four Arab/Muslim states. The president went to Turkey in April of 2009, in June of the same year he visited Saudi Arabia and Egypt, and in November 2010 he traveled to Indonesia. For most Israelis, skipping Israel three times was nothing short of a slap in the face, especially in light of the fact that the president made a solution to the conflict a top priority by appointing former Senate Majority Leader George Mitchell as a Special Envoy to the region only two days after his inauguration. To demonstrate his seriousness about the urgent need for a solution, the next president must visit Israel and the Palestinian Authority and make it abundantly clear where the U.S. stands.

Nonetheless, President Obama—throughout his presidency and recently reiterated in his speech at the U.N. General Assembly—has insisted that the only solution to the Arab-Israeli conflict rests on creating two independent states, a Jewish and a Palestinian state living side-by-side in peace while growing and prospering together as neighbors. Any other message coming from the White House, regardless of party affiliation, will fundamentally be injurious to both the Israelis and the Palestinians. The notion from some American politicians who have said that the U.S. should not have a greater desire for peace than the parties to the conflict is shortsighted. The U.S. has serious stakes in the region and responsibility toward its allies. The lack of peace will continue to undermine the U.S.' interest, erode its influence and jeopardize its role in shaping the outcome of the multiple upheavals sweeping the region in the wake of the Arab Spring.

What the U.S. President Should Do

To advance the prospect for peace between Israel and Palestine, the next president must take a number of critical steps. First, within a few months after the election, the president should visit Israel and Palestine and directly address the Israeli people as well as the Palestinians, strongly suggesting that only peace will serve their greater interests. He must look into the eyes of the Israeli and Palestinian public and emphasize that the U.S. is committed to a two-state solution and will remain consistent and resilient until such a resolution is achieved. The president should also accentuate that the U.S. will use all means available at its disposal to advance the two-state solution and stress that further delay would only harden the many facts on the ground, especially the expansion of settlements, becoming irreversible and rendering any future peace agreement virtually impossible.

Second, the president must carry with him a general framework for an Israeli-Palestinian peace based on prior agreements negotiated between the two sides, especially those achieved in 2000 (at Camp David between Yasser Arafat and Ehud Barak) and in 2007–2008 between Ehud Olmert and Mahmoud Abbas. In both sets of these comprehensive negotiations, the two sides have been able to resolve the vast majority of the conflicting issues. In the 2007–2008 talks, then-Israeli Prime Minister Olmert stated both sides had come "very close, more than ever in the past, to complete a principle agreement that would have led to the end of the conflict." These prior agreements should be placed on the table anew and modified in order to create a clear basis for negotiating a peace agreement with the U.S.' direct participation.

Third, to increase the framework's effectiveness, a new internationally recognized special envoy of the caliber of President [Bill] Clinton should be appointed with a clear *presidential mandate* to work relentlessly to advance the negotiating process while keeping a top level American official in the region to press on with the negotiations during the occasional absence of the special envoy. To avoid deadlocks, the rules of engagement should be based on an incremental agreement on various conflicting issues, ideally starting with borders. The

Palestinians should abandon their precondition to freeze the settlements before they enter the negotiating process. An agreement on borders will in and of itself resolve 70 to 80 percent of the final status of the settlements and define the parameters of the Palestinian state. Such an agreement will also facilitate the negotiations of other conflicting issues, including the status of Palestinian refugees, Jerusalem, and Israel's national security. Finally, the negotiations should not be open-ended; a timeline must be established, albeit with some flexibility, to prevent either party from playing for time.

Fourth, it is imperative that the U.S. reaches out to other leading Arab and Muslim states such as Saudi Arabia, Qatar and Turkey, to exert pressure on the Palestinian Authority to make necessary concessions. Egypt must also be approached about beginning the process of influencing Hamas to change its open enmity towards and hardline policy against Israel. In particular, the Egyptian Muslim Brotherhood–led government should persuade [militant Palestinian party] Hamas to renounce violence as a tool by which to reach its political objective of establishing an independent Palestinian state and remove from its charter the clause that calls for Israel's destruction. These Arab states, especially Egypt, have serious stakes in finding a solution to the Israeli-Palestinian conflict. Indeed, any new conflagration between Israel and the Palestinians will impact directly and indirectly not only on their interests, but could also draw them into the conflict which they want to avoid at all costs given their own internal political combustion and uncertainty.

Changing the Narrative

Fifth, once the Israelis and Palestinians engage in negotiations, the U.S. should press both to immediately begin the process of changing their public narratives about each other by mutually ending acrimonious statements and expressions of hatred and

"Peace Table," cartoon by Steve Greenberg. Copyright © by Steve Greenberg. Reproduction rights obtainable from www.CartoonStock.com.

distrust. To that end both governments should encourage universities, nonpartisan think tanks and media outlets to deliberate publicly about the psychological dimensions of the conflicting issue and begin a process of changing mindsets about some of the inevitabilities of reaching an agreement.

Even when the leaders reach an agreement behind closed doors, they cannot simply come out with pronouncements of concessions that were made by either side without first preparing the public. For example, an agreement on Palestinian refugees will of necessity entail the return of only a small fraction of refugees to Israel proper under family reunification, when in fact the vast majority of Palestinians still believe in the right of return. Additionally, there can be no two-state solution without Jerusalem becoming the capital of Israel and Palestine, albeit the city will remain united, which will be difficult for the Israeli public to accept. For these reasons, changing public perception about each conflicting issue is central to ratifying any peace accord.

Revive the API

Sixth, in reaching out to the Arab and Muslim world, the president should help reignite the Arab Peace Initiative (API) which still represents the most comprehensive solution to the Arab-Israeli conflict. The revival of the API remains critically important as even top Israeli officials, including the former head of the Israeli Mossad, Meir Dagan, have stated that the plan is central to resolving the Arab-Israeli conflict. As the whole region undergoes revolutionary change in the wake of the Arab Spring, restarting the API will have special importance in reaching a comprehensive peace and long-term stability. The creation of a "sovereign, independent Palestinian state," which the API calls for, will greatly contribute to stabilizing the region. Indeed, various Arab and Muslim countries will begin to normalize relations with Israel and foster a lasting peace that will ultimately improve the lives of millions of ordinary citizens throughout the region.

The Arab-Israeli conflict has been overshadowed in recent months by international concerns over Iran's nuclear program, the bloody civil war which continues to rage in Syria and the unending insurgencies and terrorism that continues to plague many nations. Meanwhile, the Israeli-Palestinian conflict is quietly simmering underneath the surface and is becoming ever more perilous. Israel continues to expand existing settlements and legalize others while the Palestinians remain hopelessly factionalized and aimless, unable to present a unified front to be taken seriously, and thus, leaving the festering conflict in the hands of radicals on both sides.

For either President Obama or Mitt Romney, finding a solution to the Israeli-Palestinian conflict should remain a top priority. The status quo is explosive and it can only lead to a new violent and death-defying confrontation that will leave no victors behind but will result in horrifying destruction and will irreparably deepen the already existing divide between the two sides.

The United States has both the interest and the responsibility to put an end to the Israeli-Palestinian self-consuming conflict in a region where the stakes for all concerned cannot be overestimated.

> "If there were any warmth left in our hearts, then we would all be doing everything that we possibly could do to stop Israel's crimes against the Palestinian people."

The United States Should Be Doing More to Stop Israel's Crimes Against the Palestinian People

Sarah Marusek

Sarah Marusek is a member of the International Executive Committee of the Global March to Jerusalem. In the following viewpoint, she describes her experiences in Gaza in 2013 as part of peaceful demonstrations to draw attention to Israel's continued violations against Jerusalem and its people. Marusek was both disheartened and inspired by her visit: disheartened to see people struggling to survive under a brutal Israeli occupation, and inspired to find vibrant communities and resilient people. She concludes that the Palestinian people deserve more from the international community, especially when it comes to holding Israel to account for its oppression of the Palestinian people.

As you read, consider the following questions:

1. According to Marusek, when did the second annual Global March to Jerusalem occur?

2. When did the Miles of Smiles convoy reached Gaza, as related by the author?

3. How many students does the author estimate that Islamic University educates every year?

In the eyes of many Westerners, Gaza is a dangerous and war torn place. Even activists, including myself, often imagine Gaza primarily as a place of suffering, and one that has unfairly come to eclipse the affliction of all of Palestine. But while Israel's wars of aggression against the people of Gaza, as well as its brutal siege, have cost many lives and inflicted countless casualties, Gaza today is a remarkably calm, protected and beautiful place where everyday lives go on, despite the continued suffering of its people. Indeed, Gaza is a place where the heart and soul flourish even if the body is ailing; where people and community are so alive and resilient that it rekindles one's hope in humanity.

The Global March to Jerusalem

I only know this now because I traveled to Gaza earlier this month to participate in the second annual Global March to Jerusalem (GMJ) on Friday, 7th June 2013, when thousands of Palestinians and international activists mobilized in peaceful demonstrations around the world to draw attention to Israel's continued violations against Jerusalem and its people. Although Israeli police violently suppressed GMJ demonstrations in Jerusalem and throughout the West Bank, peaceful mass demonstrations did successfully take place in Gaza and the neighboring countries of Jordan and Egypt, as well as in Tunisia, Mauritania, Morocco, Yemen, Malaysia, and Turkey.

In addition, there were demonstrations in solidarity with the GMJ all around the world, including several major cities across Europe and North America.

On Friday, 7th June I was fortunate enough to join Palestinians and a group of international activists in a peaceful mass rally in Beit Hanoun, the nearest point possible to Jerusalem in Gaza. Many thousands attended the rally, and during my address I promised to carry their voices back home with me to the US in order to communicate their struggle to live under the footprint of a racist occupying power that my government funds and arms. Of course, the few days I spent in Gaza are hardly enough to fulfill this promise. There are too many voices that I was not able to hear, both because there was not enough time and because of my identity as an American woman. But I am hoping that what I can offer begins to communicate the complex life stories of a people resisting against horrific injustices, while at the same time encouraging other Westerners to travel to Gaza in order to do the same.

Miles of Smiles

My entry into Gaza was made possible by the Miles of Smiles convoy organized by the International Committee for Breaking the Siege on Gaza (ICBSG). While there have been many international convoys entering Gaza in recent years, all of which bring much needed aid to the besieged people of Gaza, the Miles of Smiles convoy offers something unique by focusing on development aid. The first Miles of Smiles convoy reached Gaza in November 2009, and since then the ICBSG has successfully organized twenty additional convoys into Gaza. Our convoy included activists from Jordan, Egypt, Tunisia, Libya, Yemen, Saudi Arabia, Bahrain, Malaysia, South Africa, the UK, and the USA.

Miles of Smiles works closely with Partners for Peace and Development for Palestinians (PPDP) to sponsor projects that empower Palestinians to develop the means to live dignified lives on their own terms. The PPDP is a UK-based organization that works with a dedicated team of Palestinian employees and volunteers in Gaza to offer interest-free loans and small grants to Palestinians, helping them to establish family businesses and development projects. One example of this is a small bakery that we visited during the first night we spent in Gaza, which thanks to a PPDP loan generates employment for an entire family.

PPDP's Palestinian employees and volunteers in Gaza coordinated our program, which included many different activities that allowed us access to a diverse array of Palestinian voices and experiences. For example, our second day in Gaza we met with the children and spouses of Palestinians who are currently imprisoned by the occupation authorities, often without any formal charges ever being brought against them. And even when Palestinians are tried, it is in military courts—an apartheid system of justice that separates Palestinian children from their fathers, mothers, brothers, and sisters.

A Lack of Resources

Earlier that day we also visited a government hospital that specializes in caring for children. We asked one of the doctors there what the needs of the hospital are, and his answer was a lack of resources—a problem that more international activists could easily help alleviate if the US and Europe did not impose such draconian penalties for working with Hamas, the ruling party of the government in Gaza that Israel and its Western allies label as a terrorist organization because of its resistance activities against the occupation. The doctor explained to us that they have many doctors, in fact too many to employ. Even during Israel's recent war against Gaza in November of last year they had a sea of volunteers to help. However the hospital still needed equipment and medication to meet the needs of their patients. Indeed according to the hu-

Number of Persons in Gaza Killed by Israel Occupation Forces by District, 2000–2012

Year	North Gaza	Gaza	Deir Al Balah	Khan Younis	Rafah	Total
2000	8	52	16	19	28	123
2001	40	65	34	52	52	243
2002	70	108	70	97	125	472
2003	89	118	75	42	72	398
2004	181	162	53	100	149	646
2005	34	10	13	20	22	99
2006	236	145	45	51	57	534
2007	81	69	50	58	23	281
2008	211	256	131	107	64	769
2009	440	450	68	64	36	1058
2010	14	16	16	16	10	72
2011	15	43	10	15	27	112
2012	52	96	47	32	25	252
Total	1471	1590	628	673	690	5059

In addition to the above mentioned number, there were two Egyptians killed in 2001, an American and British persons killed in 2003, a British person killed in 2004, and two Egyptian persons killed in 2011.

TAKEN FROM: Al Mezan Center for Human Rights, 2013.

man rights organization B'Tselem, Israeli forces killed 167 Palestinians during last November's military operation, at least 87 of them civilians and more than one third under the age of 18. As we visited some of the sick children I felt so helpless and angry because as an American I am unable to contribute anything to the important work of this hospital, which saves innocent children's lives. Fortunately, those in Arab countries are able to donate without fear of prosecution, and their contributions help keep the hospital running.

Islamic University

On our fourth day we visited Islamic University, the best university in Gaza (there are seven in total) and ranked among the top 250 universities around the world. Founded in 1978, the university's campus is modern and beautiful, servicing around 20,000 students each year. The university offers many degrees across the arts and sciences, with Islamic values guiding the behavior of the students as well as the curriculum, which is in line with international scientific standards. But even this university has suffered unjustly under the occupation. During Israel's December 2008 war against Gaza, occupation forces destroyed 74 of the university's laboratories, as well as a library, a collective punishment against the entire population. Lest anybody think that this was collateral damage, Israel deliberately bombed the university in six separate air strikes. When I think of violent acts that would terrorize me as a teacher and a scholar, this ranks among the worst. And yet this terrorism is exactly what my government is uncritically supporting.

During our time in Gaza, we also met with Prime Minister Ismael Haniyeh, and distributed aid to orphans as well as to needy families thanks to the generosity of our Libyan delegation (as well as my own friends and colleagues who kindly donated money so that I could distribute toys to children). But most of us will never really know what it is like to live under a violent occupation. What it is like to be cruelly besieged by your neighbor and demonized by Western countries for fighting back. We spoke to some graduates of Islamic University who are involved in the Gaza student community, to try and learn more about their own experiences.

Holding Back Their Anger

One member of the convoy, an American filmmaker of Pakistani origin, remarked how surprising it was that the Palestinians working with us were not more angry. One young man responded that, in fact, they are very angry, but that they still have to live. He explained that he holds his pain and suffering deep inside himself, as do other Palestinians in Gaza. It has to be contained for fear that if expressed it could destroy their lives. And even though he spoke these words calmly and quietly, the inner anguish distorted his face and the grief filled his wide eyes. He told us that he lost seven friends in the last war against his people. On his way to sit for his university exams he also saw bombs destroy the buildings around him. His exams were postponed. But what really made the suffering intolerable was getting through the cold nights during that war.

I can only conclude that this coldness is symbolic of a world where an occupying power can terrorize and ethnically cleanse a native population with impunity. Because if there were any warmth left in our hearts, then we would all be doing everything that we possibly could do to stop Israel's crimes against the Palestinian people. Convoys like Miles of Smiles help, as do solidarity activities like the GMJ, but considering the extent of their suffering, the Palestinians deserve more from all of us.

Periodical and Internet Sources Bibliography

The following articles have been selected to supplement the diverse views presented in this chapter.

Reza Aslan	"Yes to Palestine," *Los Angeles Times*, September 15, 2011.
Boston Globe	"Palestinian Authority's Woes Are a Problem for US, Israel," October 1, 2012.
Kevin Flower	"What Does Palestinian Statehood Bid Mean?," CNN.com, September 26, 2011.
HDS Greenway	"Obama Should Support Palestinian Statehood," Global Post, September 20, 2011. www.globalpost.com.
Joshua Hersh	"US Takes Lonely Path in Opposing All Forms of Palestinian Recognition," *Huffington Post*, September 15, 2011. www.huffingtonpost.com.
Nadia Hijab	"Rethinking Aid to Palestine," *Foreign Policy*, August 3, 2012.
John B. Judis	"Why the US Should Support Palestinian Statehood at the UN," *New Republic*, September 28, 2011.
Joseph Klein	"US Aid Funding Palestinian Terrorism," *FrontPage*, April 22, 2013.
Michael Lerner	"Why US, Israel Should Welcome Palestinian Move at the UN," CNN.com, November 29, 2012.
David B. Rivkin Jr. and Lee A. Casey	"The Legal Case Against Palestinian Statehood," *Wall Street Journal*, September 20, 2011.
Pierre Tristam	"US on Wrong Side of History with Vote Against Palestine," *Fort Lauderdale (FL) Sun-Sentinel*, December 4, 2012.

For Further Discussion

Chapter 1

1. *The Economist* contends that a two-state solution to the Israeli-Palestinian conflict would be logical and successful. Ghada Karmi suggests that a one-state solution is more workable. After reading both viewpoints, which solution do you believe should be implemented in the region and why?

2. How does Anne-Marie Slaughter define two-state condominialism? What do you think of it as a solution to the Palestinian/Israeli conflict?

3. In recent discussions regarding a two-state solution, there has been much debate on the details of a Palestinian state. One of the most heated has been on its borders. In his viewpoint, Barack Obama underscores the need to establish Palestine on pre-1967 borders. George Berkin argues that this is unrealistic and will never happen. Which author makes the more convincing argument and why?

Chapter 2

1. After reading all viewpoints in the chapter, discuss your conclusions regarding whether the United Nations should (or even can) grant Palestinian statehood. Why would it be a good idea to allow Palestinian statehood? Why would it be a bad move?

2. In her viewpoint, Hillary Clinton argues that Palestinian statehood is counterproductive and will block peace efforts. Do you think that she is correct? Or do you agree with Pierre Tristam that it is the right thing to do, despite the obstacles? Explain.

Chapter 3

1. Should the Palestinian Authority be dissolved? Read viewpoints by Steven A. Cook and Dawoud Abu Lebdeh to inform your answer.

2. Jeff Jacoby asserts that the Palestinian Authority should recognize Israel as a Jewish state. After reading the viewpoint, do you find his argument convincing? Why?

3. The reconciliation of Hamas and Fatah inspired a range of reaction across the political spectrum. James Zogby viewed it as a positive development for the Palestinian people and crucial to the peace process with Israel. Michael Rubin was skeptical of that view and argued that it could threaten prospects for peace. What is your opinion on the Hamas-Fatah reconciliation and its effect on the peace process? Use information from the viewpoints to support your position.

4. Is Fayyadism a viable and effective way to strengthen prospects for a two-state solution? Some political leaders consider Fayyadism, the movement to build and strengthen Palestinian institutions, essential to a future Palestinian state. Nathan J. Brown refutes that idea. Cite from the viewpoint to inform your answer.

Chapter 4

1. Zvi Bar'el maintains that the United States should recognize Palestinian statehood. In his viewpoint, John R. Bolton argues that the United States should not do so. Which author makes the better argument and why?

2. After reading all six viewpoints in the chapter, do you believe brokering peace between Israel and Palestine should be the highest priority for the United States? What should be the goal of the United States regarding the Palestinian territories, and how should it pursue that goal?

Organizations to Contact

The editors have compiled the following list of organizations concerned with the issues debated in this book. The descriptions are derived from materials provided by the organizations. All have publications or information available for interested readers. The list was compiled on the date of publication of the present volume; the information provided here may change. Be aware that many organizations take several weeks or longer to respond to inquiries, so allow as much time as possible.

Al Mezan Center for Human Rights

PO Box 5270 5/102-1 Al-Mena, Omar El-Mukhtar St.
Gaza City, Gaza Strip
+972 (0)8 282-0447
e-mail: info@mezan.org
website: www.mezan.org

The Al Mezan Center for Human Rights is a Palestinian human rights organization that is devoted to the idea of a sovereign Palestinian state characterized by good governance, economic and social justice, vibrant democratic institutions and citizen participation, and the rule of law. The center works to protect the human rights of citizens in the Palestinian Territories, particularly the Gaza Strip, as well as the collective rights of the Palestinian people. It trains activists, schoolteachers, and community leaders in human rights law; monitors and documents human rights violations in the Palestinian Territories; provides legal representation for political prisoners, victims of home confiscation, and others; and offers resources in marginalized areas, like refugee camps, to help and protect the rights of Palestinians. The center's website features statistics on home demolitions, deaths, and reported human rights violations; position papers, speeches and testimony transcripts; legal references; in-depth reports; and news briefs on relevant topics.

American Israel Public Affairs Committee (AIPAC)

251 H St. NW, Washington, DC   20001
(202) 639-5200
website: www.aipac.org

Founded in 1963, AIPAC is a pro-Israel advocacy group that "empowers pro-Israel activists across all ages, religions and races to be politically engaged and build relationships with members of Congress from both sides of the aisle to promote the US-Israel relationship." AIPAC builds relationships with religious leaders, politicians and policy makers, college students, and activists to fight anti-Semitism; facilitate a better understanding of Israel and threats to its security; foster economic, social, and political bonds between the United States and Israel; and lobby members of the US Congress to support Israeli policies. The group is committed to advancing its position on a number of issues, including Hamas, Palestinian statehood, Israeli settlements in the Palestinian Territories, and others. The AIPAC website provides access to speeches and testimony from key AIPAC officials, as well as to several publications, including *AIPAC Memo*, an analysis of current issues; *Defense Digest*, a monthly compilation of articles on Israel's security; and the *Middle East Spotlight*, an analysis of Middle East events that could impact US-Israel relations.

American Jewish Committee (AJC)

165 E. Fifty-Sixth St., New York, NY   10022
(212) 751-4000
website: www.ajc.org

The American Jewish Committee is a Jewish advocacy group that works for the well-being of the Jewish people and Israel as well as the advancement of the peace process in Israel and the Palestinian Territories. The AJC supports bilateral peace negotiations between Israel and the Palestinians, insists that the Palestinians recognize Israel as a Jewish state, and rejects the right of return for Palestinian refugees. The AJC mobilizes the support of Jewish Americans in support of these positions, and lobbies US policy makers and diplomatic voices to adopt these views. The AJC is also very active in a number of other areas, including the fight against global anti-Semitism and advancing interfaith understanding. The AJC website features commentary, press releases, and a blog for readers; it also has audio and radio commentary by AJC experts that focuses on issues relevant to the Jewish community.

American Task Force on Palestine (ATFP)
1634 Eye St. NW, Ste. 725, Washington, DC   20006
(202) 887-0177 • fax: (202) 887-1920
e-mail: info@atfp.net
website: www.americantaskforce.org

The American Task Force on Palestine is a nonprofit and non-partisan organization that was created to strengthen Palestinian-American relations. The ATFP works to "articulate and educate about the United States national interest in helping to create a Palestinian state living alongside Israel in peace, security and dignity." To accomplish this goal, it advocates for diplomatic and legislative efforts; facilitates programs with nongovernmental organizations (NGOs), activists, and government officials that encourage peace between Israelis and Palestinians; and supports efforts to build and strengthen Palestinian institutions, including health care, education, and good governance. The ATFP website features information on recent campaigns, breaking news, ATFP position papers, press releases, and commentary, and video of key speeches and interviews of Palestinian officials.

Americans for Peace Now (APN)
2100 M. St. NW, Ste. 619, Washington, DC   20037
(202) 408-9898 • fax: (202) 408-9899
e-mail: apndc@peacenow.org
website: peacenow.org

Americans for Peace Now was established in 1981 to mobilize support for the peace movement in Israel. Today, it is one of the largest American organizations working for peace between Israel and the Palestinian Territories. APN's website offers a range of resources, including a blog, recent news stories from Israeli media, a recommended reading list, audio, video, and an events calendar. It also provides access to both the congressional and legislative briefing books, which offer information important to a better understanding of the Israeli-Palestinian conflict and the challenges of forging a lasting peace in the region.

Foundation for Middle East Peace (FMEP)

1761 N St. NW, Washington, DC   20036
(202) 835-3650 • fax: (202) 835-3651
e-mail: info@fmep.org
website: www.fmep.org

The Foundation for Middle East Peace is a nonprofit organization that is dedicated to find a way to forge a lasting peace between Israel and Palestine. To this end, FMEP offers small grants to support educational, civil rights, recreational, and humanitarian activities that promote peace and a greater understanding of the issues involved in the conflict. Since 1992 FMEP has published the *Report on Israeli Settlements in the Occupied Territories*, a bimonthly periodical that features detailed and insightful analysis on the Israeli-Palestinian issue. Commentary and analysis on a range of topics related to the conflict can be accessed on the FMEP website.

The Israeli Committee Against House Demolitions (ICAHD)

PO Box 2030, Jerusalem   91020
   Israel
+972 2 622-1530 • fax: +972 2 624-5560
e-mail: info@icahd.org
website: www.icahd.org

Established in 1997, the Israeli Committee Against House Demolitions is a human rights and peace organization that works to end Israel's occupation of the Palestinian Territories. The central goal of the ICAHD is to stop the Israeli government's policy of demolishing Palestinian homes in the Occupied Territories and in Israel, regarding this destructive policy as a serious human rights violation that also destroys long-standing communities and cultural and social bonds. The ICAHD website offers access to a range of resources, including films, news and updates, webinars, statistics, maps, commentary, and reports on specific issues. Publications available on the group's website include *Demolishing Homes, Demolishing Peace* and *A Policy of Displacement: Visualizing Palestine*.

The Middle East Institute (MEI)

1761 N St. NW, Washington, DC   20036
(202) 785-1141 • fax: (202) 331-8861
e-mail: information@mei.edu
website: www.mei.edu

The Middle East Institute was established in 1946 to provide unbiased and insightful information on the Middle East and facilitate a better understanding of the region for US policy makers, business leaders, and students. The MEI hosts lectures and conferences that feature regional experts from around the world and offer a variety of views on topical issues. It also provides accredited classes in Arabic, Hebrew, Persian, and Turkish languages, culture, and history and publishes the *Middle East Journal*, a journal that includes scholarly research and cogent analysis on Middle East issues and US–Middle East relations. There are several other publications available on the MEI website, including *Policy Brief*, which comprises analytical writings by MEI scholars and other experts on a wide range of subjects, and *Viewpoints*, which contain debates between experts that offer differing perspectives on current issues.

The Middle East Policy Council (MEPC)

1730 M St. NW, Ste. 512, Washington, DC   20036
(202) 296-6767
e-mail: info@mepc.org
website: www.mepc.org

The Middle East Policy Council is a nonprofit educational organization established in 1981 to inform the debate on political, cultural, and economic issues of US interest in the Middle

East, such as the Arab Spring, the Israel-Palestinian conflict, and Islamic fundamentalism and global jihad. MEPC organizes the Capitol Hill conference series, which brings together regional analysts and congressional staffs for a discussion of key political issues. It also publishes *Middle East Policy*, a quarterly journal that reports on and analyzes a wide range of subjects related to the Middle East and US foreign policy in the region. A number of articles and commentary by MEPC scholars can be accessed on the organization's website.

National Council on US-Arab Relations (NCUSAR)

1730 M St. NW, Ste. 503, Washington, DC   20036
(202) 293-6466 • fax: (202) 283-7770
website: www.ncusar.org

The National Council on US-Arab Relations is a nonprofit educational organization that was established in 1983 to inform American understanding of the Arab world. NCUSAR offers study abroad opportunities for eligible students; coordinates the Model Arab League, a program in which students learn about Arab history and geopolitical interests; and oversees the Malone Fellowship in Arab and Islamic Studies. NCUSAR also holds public educational briefings on Capitol Hill to debate and exchange ideas on US foreign policy in the Middle East and ways to improve US-Arab relations. The NCUSAR website features a range of articles, commentaries, policy briefs, videos, and newsletters, including the *Council Chronicle* and *NCUSAR Newsletter*.

US Department of State

2201 C St. NW, Washington, DC   20520
(202) 647-4000
website: www.state.gov

The US Department of State is the federal agency that is responsible for formulating, implementing, and assessing US foreign policy. The State Department also assists US citizens living or traveling abroad, promotes and protects US business interests all over the world, and supports the activities of other US federal agencies in foreign countries. The State Department is central in enacting diplomatic efforts to resolve the Israeli-Palestinian conflict and informing the US Congress, the president, and the public about the political, economic, and social events in the region. The State Department website features a wealth of information on current policies, upcoming events, daily schedules of top officials, and updates from various countries. It also has video, congressional testimony, speech transcripts, background notes, human rights reports, and strategy reviews.

Bibliography of Books

Yasmeen Abu-Laban and Abigail B. Bakan — *Israel, Palestine, and the Politics of Race: Exploring Identity and Power in a Global Context.* New York: I. B. Tauris, 2014.

Emanuel Adler, ed. — *Israel in the World: Legitimacy and Exceptionalism.* New York: Routledge, 2013.

Daniel Baracskay — *The Palestinian Liberation Organization: Terrorism and Prospects for Peace in the Holy Land.* Santa Barbara, CA: 2011.

Dan Bavly and As'ad Ghanem — *One State, Two Peoples: Restoring Hope for Palestinian-Israeli Peace.* Dulles, VA: Potomac, 2013.

Ian J. Bickerton — *Arab-Israeli Conflict: A Guide for the Perplexed.* New York: Continuum, 2012.

Dale Hanson Bourke — *The Israeli-Palestinian Conflict: Tough Questions, Direct Answers.* Downers Grove, IL: IVP, 2013.

Richard Cohen — *Israel: Can It Survive?* New York: Simon & Schuster, 2014.

William A. Cook, ed. — *Plight of the Palestinians: A Long History of Destruction.* New York: Palgrave Macmillan, 2010.

Rochelle Davis and Mimi Kirk, eds. — *Palestine and the Palestinians in the 21st Century.* Bloomington: Indiana University Press, 2013.

Alan Dowty — *Israel/Palestine.* Malden, MA: Polity, 2012.

Norman G. Finkelstein — *'This Time We Went Too Far': Truth and Consequences of the Gaza Invasion.* New York: OR, 2010.

James L. Gelvin — *The Israel-Palestine Conflict: One Hundred Years of War.* 3rd ed. New York: Cambridge University Press, 2014.

Hirsh Goodman — *The Anatomy of Israel's Survival.* New York: PublicAffairs, 2011.

Mustafa Kabha — *The Palestinian People: Seeking Sovereignty and State.* Boulder, CO: Lynne Rienner, 2013.

Rashid Khalidi — *Brokers of Deceit: How the US Has Undermined Peace in the Middle East.* Boston: Beacon, 2013.

Michael Lerner — *Embracing Israel/Palestine: A Strategy to Heal and Transform the Middle East.* Berkeley, CA: North Atlantic, 2011.

Rene H. Levy — *Baseless Hatred: What It Is and What You Can Do About It.* Lynbrook, NY: Gefen, 2011.

Moshe Machover — *Israelis and Palestinians: Conflict and Resolution.* Chicago: Haymarket, 2011.

Thomas G. Mitchell — *Israel/Palestine and the Politics of a Two-State Solution.* Jefferson, NC: McFarland, 2013.

Joshua Muravchik	*Making David into Goliath: How the World Turned Against Israel.* New York: Encounter, 2014.
Wendy Pearlman	*Violence, Nonviolence, and the Palestinian National Movement.* New York: Cambridge University Press, 2011.
Ilan Peleg and Dov Waxman	*Israel's Palestinians: The Conflict Within.* New York: Cambridge University Press, 2011.
Ari Shavit	*My Promised Land: The Triumph and Tragedy of Israel.* New York: Spiegel & Grau, 2013.
Asher Susser	*Israel, Jordan, and Palestine: The Two-State Imperative.* Waltham, MA: Brandeis University Press, 2012.
Virginia Tilley, ed.	*Beyond Occupation: Apartheid, Colonialism and International Law in the Occupied Palestinian Territories.* New York: Palgrave Macmillan, 2012.

Index